Psychoanalysis

A SUN BOOK

WALKER SUN BOOKS

SB-1 *Islam* by Dominique Sourdel

SB-2 *Africa Before the White Man* by Henri Labouret

SB-3 *War* by Gaston Bouthoul

SB-4 *Buddhism* by Henri Arvon

SB-5 *The Nature of Hinduism* by Louis Renou

SB-6 *The Essence of Ancient Philosophy* by André Cresson

SB-7 *A History of Alchemy* by Serge Hutin

SB-8 *Surrealism* by Yves Duplessis

SB-9 *The Churches of the West* by Marcel Pacaut

SB-10 *A History of Judaism* by André Chouraqui

SB-11 *A History of Magic* by Jérôme-Antoine Rony

SB-12 *Socrates* by Jean Brun

SB-13 *Hitler's Germany* by Claude David

SB-14 *Sexual Reproduction* by Louis Gallien

SB-15 *Memory and Forgetting* by Jean-Claude Filloux

SB-16 *Aerodynamics* by Jacques Lachnitt

SB-17 *Psychoanalysis* by Daniel Lagache

SB-18 *Longevity* by Jacques Guillerme

SB-19 *The Psychology of Animals* by Jean-Claude Filloux

SB-20 *Probability and Certainty* by Emile Borel

SB-21 *Nuclear Radiations* by Marc Lefort

SB-22 *The Earth and the Moon* by Jean Taille

SB-23 *The Origins of Life* by Jules Carles

SB-24 *Animal Migration* by René Thévenin

Psychoanalysis

DANIEL LAGACHE

Professor at the Sorbonne;
President, French Psychoanalytic Society

Translated by Beatrice Scott

A SUN BOOK

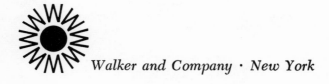
Walker and Company · New York

First published in France as LA PSYCHANALYSE. © 1955,
Presses Universitaires de France.

Copyright © this translation 1963 by Walker and
Company, a division of Publications Development
Corporation.

Published simultaneously in Canada by George J.
McLeod, Limited, Toronto.

Library of Congress Catalog Card Number: 62–19507
Manufactured in the United States of America

Contents

Introduction   1

1. The Historical Aspects   3

*The Pre-Psychoanalytic Era · Freud (1856–1939) ·
The Invention of Psychoanalysis · The First Theories
· The Development of Psychoanalysis (1905–1920) ·
Theoretical Modifications · Present-Day Tendencies*

2. Psychoanalytic Perspectives   15

3. Fundamental Principles   18

*Definition · The Principle of Constancy · The Princi-
ple of Pleasure-Unpleasure · The Reality Principle ·
Repetition Compulsion · Links with Psychology*

4. Impulses   25

*Definition · The First Theory of the Impulses · Nar-
cissism · The Second Theory of the Impulses · The
Maturation of the Impulses · The Education of the Impulses*

5. The Personality   34

*General Aspects · The First Theory of the Psychic Ap-
paratus · The Second Theory of the Psychic Apparatus
· The Genesis of the Personality*

6. Behavior   42

*General Aspects · Motivation · The Elaboration of
Behavior · Research on Methods · Objects · Dis-
charge and Defense · The Secondary Effects of Behavior
· Consciousness and Unconsciousness · Behavior and
Communication*

7. Everyday Life   51

Psychoanalysis and Everyday Life · *Slips and Errors*

8. Sleep, Dreams and Nightmares   55

Sleep and Insomnia · *The Dream* · *The Painful Dream and the Nightmare*

9. Psychic Disorders   65

The Functional Concept of Behavioral Disorders · *Psychoneuroses* · *The Classification of Neuroses* · *The Cause of Psychoneuroses* · *The Formation of Psychoneurotic Symptoms* · *Psychoses* · *Perversions* · *Character Neuroses* · *Criminal Behavior*

10. Somatic Disorders   87

Historical Comments · *Conversion Hysteria* · *Vegetative Neuroses* · *Somatic Illnesses* · *Practical Problems*

11. Psychoanalytic Treatment   95

General Remarks · *Initial Interviews* · *External Conditions of Treatment* · *The Fundamental Rule* · *The Analyst's Role* · *Transference and the Transference Neurosis* · *Therapeutic Achievements* · *Healing Mechanisms*

12. Variations in Psychoanalytic Treatment   108

Plasticity or Rigidity · *The Psychoanalysis of Children* · *Psychoanalysis of the Psychoses* · *The Psychoanalysis of Criminals* · *Conclusions*

13. Psychoanalysis and Psychotherapy   115

Similarities and Differences · *Hypnosis and Suggestion* · *The Problem of Short Treatment* · *Group Psychoanalysis* · *Psychoanalysis and Theatrotherapy* · *Psychotherapy under Narcosis*

14. Psychoanalytic Research   125

Psychoanalysis as "Action-Research" · *The Psychoanalytic Field* · *Analytic Material* · *The Genesis of Interpretation* · *The Validity of Interpretations*

15. Psychoanalysis and the Humanities   131

16. Psychoanalysis and Morals   136

17. The Psychoanalyst   139

Bibliography   143

Index   145

Introduction

There is a tendency for the general public to use the word *psychoanalysis* vaguely. In fact, this term cannot legitimately be applied to anything except the research methods and treatment invented by Freud, and the theories that derive from these. This is recognized by the divergent schools that have invented special terms to designate their own doctrines and methods, such as the "analytical psychology" of Jung and the "individual psychology" of Adler.

To Freud himself, writing in 1922, the term psychoanalysis implied three things: a method of investigating mental processes almost inaccessible to all other methods; a technique for the treatment of neurotic disorders based on this method of investigation; and a body of psychological knowledge the accumulation of which leads toward the creation of a new scientific discipline.

When we are concerned with psychoanalysis as such, it is convenient to distinguish the application of psychoanalytic concepts in different fields of the human sciences and psychological practice. In the absence of psychoanalytic research we are left here with a set of hypotheses the validity of which is in no way guaranteed by their origin. In the last resort validity depends on methods of verification appropriate to the field of practical application in question.

1 / The Historical Aspects

The Pre-Psychoanalytic Era

Psychoanalysis was born in the last decade of the nineteenth century. The preceding decade had been a fertile one for psychological medicine and had been distinguished by various achievements that coincided with the advent of psychoanalysis.

Chronologically we come first to the case of Anna O., who was treated by Dr. Joseph Breuer of Vienna between 1880 and 1882. The case history was not published until 1895 (in *Studies in Hysteria*, by Breuer and Freud), but it was known to Freud long before this.

The patient was a hysteric, twenty-one years old and very intelligent. Her symptoms included contraction of the limbs with anesthesia on the left side and sometimes on the right; disorder of ocular motility and vision; difficulty in holding the head straight; a severe nervous cough; anorexia and inability to drink despite intense thirst; and states of "absence." The neurosis had begun when the young girl was looking after her father, whom she adored, during an illness of which he eventually died, thus forcing her to stop her care of him.

Breuer observed his patient with great attention, and noticed that during her "absences" she would murmur words that seemed to refer to her most intimate preoccupations. He put her into a hypnotic trance and repeated these words to her. The patient then repeated the words also, and verbalized sad daydreams the subject of which was a young girl at the bedside of her sick father. When she had given expression to a certain number of these daydreams, she found she was free and could return to a normal existence. This improvement would disappear on the next day and then return after another hypnotic session. The patient, who always spoke English, kept referring to "a talking cure or chimney sweeping." The symptoms would disappear when she had remembered the occasion of their first manifestation, and after an externalization of the emotions involved. In this way the inability to drink had come on after her governess' little dog, which she disliked, had drunk from a glass. Out of politeness she had said nothing but had suddenly become unable to drink herself: "When she had finished what she was saying, her anger, which she had contained up to then, was given violent expression. Then she asked for a drink, drank a large amount of water, and came out of the hypnotic state with the glass at her lips. The trouble had disappeared for good."

Breuer then began to study all the symptoms systematically and found that many psychic traumas could be tracked down to their origin, and that the detection of the more recent ones preceded the detection of those of longer standing. In this way all of Anna O.'s symptoms were successively cured, up to the moment when Breuer, taken by surprise at the development of a "transference" love relationship, took flight and broke off the treatment (Freud). Breuer had invented the "cathartic" treatment (from the Greek *catharsis*, purgation) under hypnosis, which he was later to study with Freud (1895).

In 1882 Jean-Martin Charcot, a clinical professor in disorders of the nervous system, produced a paper on those nervous states that could be isolated by hypnotizing hysterics: lethargy, catalepsy and somnambulism. According to Charcot and the Salpêtrière school, these states could not be observed clearly except in hysterics. The subject of hysteria and hypnosis gave rise to many papers on all sides: in 1884 and 1885 Charcot, in his lectures on hysterical paralyses, demonstrated their connection with emotional traumata, with the ideas and preoccupations the patient harbors about his physical symptoms—a concept supported by the German Moebius (1888).

The school of Nancy was more clinically and therapeutically oriented. For Bernheim (1884), hypnosis depended on a natural credulity that experience had shown most people could arrive at very easily. Less concerned with psychology, Bernheim was more interested in the practical and therapeutic effects of suggestion. In criticizing the school of Salpêtrière, Bernheim held that the three stages of hypnosis described by Charcot were a cultural artifact; and as Pierre Janet puts it, it was he who carried the day.

Janet himself had established the pathogenic effect of forgotten memories of events connected with violent emotions, in his earliest research (1886–1889); these observations are described in *Psychological Automatism* (1889).

The traumatic memory cannot be experienced in the waking state, but only if the subject is put into the somnambulistic state. When the anxiety and reticence of the patient make one suspect gaps, the treatment consists in finding out whether dreams, somnambulism or automatic writing can perhaps bring to light hidden memories. According to Janet, dissociation of memory is due to a mechanical process, to psychological weakness, and not to a dynamic process of repression.

To summarize, psychological medicine during the decade 1880–1890 was characterized by the following:

1. Interest in the nervous neuroses, and particularly in hysteria.

2. The use of hypnosis as a research method.

3. The discovery of the pathogenic effect of unconscious memories of traumatic events.

4. The therapeutic effect of hypnosis, suggestion and catharsis.

Freud (*1856–1939*)

The life of Sigmund Freud has been set down by Freud himself and by various biographers (including Sachs and Jones). Freud was born at Freiberg in Moravia in 1856. In 1860 his family moved to Vienna, where he was educated. He entered the University of Vienna in 1873. From 1876 to 1882 he was a member of Brucke's Laboratory (*Histology of the Nervous System*). In 1881 he became a doctor of medicine. He left the laboratory in 1882 to take up internal medicine and neurology. In 1884 came his engagement— just as he was on the point of discovering the anesthetic properties of cocaine, on which he was then doing research.

In 1885, a fledgling neuropathologist, he went to France for the first time and visited Charcot. After staying in Berlin for a while, he published some important work on infantile encephalopathy. In 1886 he became established as a doctor in Vienna and gave up electrotherapy for hypnosis and suggestion. In 1889 a visit to see Bernheim and Liébault at Nancy showed him more clearly the limitations of hypnosis and suggestion. It was toward the end of this decade that he began to use Breuer's method. In 1893 he published his first work, *The Psychic Mechanism of Hysterical Phenomena*. In 1895 he published *Studies in Hysteria*, with Breuer.

Freud, then, was not simply a practitioner, nor was he an empiricist. His scientific and medical knowledge places him among the best-informed neurologists of his time. In addition, he had very wide general culture and profound theoretical interests. It also seems that personal problems led him to take an interest in psychological analysis and the interpretation of dreams. All these facts played their part in the invention of psychoanalysis.

The Invention of Psychoanalysis

During the last decade of the nineteenth century Freud, in his attack on the problem of the psychological treatment of neurotics and especially hysterics, conducted a series of experiments that resulted in the invention of psychoanalysis. In the first stage he used the cathartic method in collaboration with Breuer: when the patient had been put under hypnosis, the doctor questioned him on matters connected with the origin of his symptoms, in a way calculated to allow a relevant emotional discharge. In this way the two men showed that the origin of hysterical symptoms lies in emotional upheavals belonging to the past. These disturbing events may have been completely rejected in consciousness, but they can be re-evoked in the hypnotic state.

Apart from the fact that catharsis did not produce a lasting therapeutic effect, Freud disliked hypnosis for its uncertainty, and because it smacked of magic; too, he was not able to hypnotize all his patients. This led him (during a short period between 1895 and 1899) to resort to suggestion in the waking state: the doctor, putting his hand on the patient's brow, assured him that he had the ability to remember the past. In this Freud recalled Bernheim's lesson, and showed that traumatic events are not really forgotten. But this technique is too painful: the therapist comes into conflict with the patient's resistance, and to cure him it is necessary to conquer this resistance, to conquer the repression rooted in the patient's defense of those tendencies he has that are open to criticism.

In this way there grew up the technique of training the patient to abandon the critical attitude and to interpret the material thus produced. The postulate of mental determinism implies that everything that happens after a certain point is itself connected with that point. From this is derived the "fundamental rule" of "free association," which encourages the patient to express everything, even if it seems to him unpleasant, absurd, futile or beside the point. The expression of the association of ideas is accompanied by the liberation of repressed affects. It is to the interpretation of this material—simultaneously a process of investigation and of treatment—that Freud gave the name psychoanalysis.

The discovery of transference soon completed the basic picture; a first expression of it can be found in *Studies in Hysteria* (1895) and in the analysis of Dora, finished in 1899 but only published in 1905. During the transference state, instead of simply remembering the past, the patient behaves toward the psychoanalyst as he has behaved in childhood toward those in his environment. In this way the observer, in noting the present state of affairs, is put on the trail of the past. At the same time the patient learns how to control emotions he has not been able to master in the past, and against which his only previous defense has been complete repression from consciousness.

The First Theories

For more than ten years, up to about 1906, Freud was almost the only pioneer of the new discipline. He published several basic works: *The Interpretation of Dreams* (1889), *The Psychopathology of Everyday Life* (1901), *Three Contributions to the Theory of Sex, Wit and Its Relation to the Unconscious* (1905). A coordination of his observations and views took form in his concept of the totality of mental life. Here a basic motif is the duality of the sexual impulses (which tend toward the preservation of the species) and the ego impulses (which tend toward the preservation of the individual). The function of the psychic apparatus is to reduce unpleasant tensions, either by discharge or by an intrapsychic process of defense and repression. Consciousness, then, represents only the surface of the psychic apparatus, the larger part of which is unconscious. Repressed unconscious drives seek to force their way out; for example, in dreams and neurotic symptoms.

These drives have been repressed during the development of infantile sexuality, a development that begins at birth and culminates between the ages of three and five in the Oedipus complex—the attachment of the child to the parent of the opposite sex, with a corresponding hostility toward the parent of the same sex.

The Development of Psychoanalysis (1905–1920)

The period between 1905 and 1920 is remarkable for the development of a psychoanalytic movement. From 1902 on several doctors grouped themselves about Freud; about 1906 psychoanalytic activity gained impetus at Zurich, with Bleuler and Jung; and in the following years new disciples included Ernest Jones (Toronto and later London), Karl Abraham (Berlin) and Sandor Ferenczi (Budapest).

On the whole, psychoanalysis was welcomed eagerly in Germany and with great interest in the United States and England, but was ignored in the Latin countries; the first book to come out on it in France was that of Régis and Hesnard (1914). Not until after World War I did psychoanalysis become international (1920–1922).

From the technical point of view this period was marked by a growing conviction of the importance of resistance and transference. Most of Freud's technical works were published between 1912 and 1919; psychoanalytic information became more precise; and it became necessary to institute training analyses. The organization of this body of knowledge gave central importance in the pathogenesis of the neuroses to the developmental anomalies of the Oedipus complex, but this was also the period in which ego psychology first appeared (cf. Freud's *Introduction to Nar-*

cissism, 1914). Two defections occurred in 1911, those of Adler and Jung. Adler stressed the importance of aggression rather than of sexuality, and of the ego rather than the unconscious. Jung, on the other hand, with his interest in morality and religion, set the collective unconscious up against the individual unconscious, and favored a symbolic interpretation of the Oedipus complex rather than a sexual one. Technically, emphasis shifted from past conflict to that of the present, and intervention became more readily moralizing, as against the pure analysis of resistance and transference.

Theoretical Modifications

Already foreshadowed in earlier work, the major modifications were formulated from 1920 on. They relate especially to the theory of impulses and the theory of the psychic apparatus.

The new Freudian theory of impulses (in German, *Triebe*) opposed the life impulses (sexuality, libido, Eros) to the death impulses and aggression (Thanatos). From the very beginning psychoanalysis had recognized the importance of hate and ambivalence, but aggression had been considered secondary to frustration and subordinate to sexuality. However, progress in clinical investigations, and particularly discoveries connected with obsessions and melancholia, showed that the role of aggression had been underestimated. In *Beyond the Pleasure Principle* (1920) Freud cited repetition phenomena (children's play, traumatic neurosis, the neurosis of destiny, and transference) and certain biological considerations as evidence for the existence of a primitive self-destructive tendency. Death impulses are more basic than life impulses. By reducing tension they tend to re-establish an anterior or inorganic state; they also tend toward repetition. Death impulses are difficult to identify as such, but find their expression in the defense mechanisms, in projection outward (paranoia), in fusion with libidinal impulses (sadism, masochism), and in a turning against the ego (melancholia).

The new theory of the psychic apparatus distinguished three systems: those of the id, the ego and the superego (1923). Up to this time it had been thought sufficient to distinguish the unconscious system (which contains repressed material) and the preconscious system (with consciousness at its disposal), with the so-called censor playing its part between the two. The defense mechanisms (that is, the repressive forces) were thought to act unconsciously; things unconscious do not have to be repressed. In the new conception, the id was the seat of impulses and repressed desires; the ego, differentiated from the id by contact with reality, controlled access to perception and action; and the superego, differentiated from the ego, is formed by the internalization of idealized images of the parents, primitive love objects, during the course of Oedipal conflict; it is the basis of self-esteem and of guilt feelings. The interplay of the ego and the superego insures defense against impulses and repressed desires.

These modifications have had a considerable effect on both the theory and the practice of psychoanalysis. Whether we consider the development of the personality or the dynamics of conflict, there are two principal implications: (1) Psychoanalytic interpretations are no longer conceived in terms of impulse conflict, but in terms of the ego's defense against impulses and emotions; (2) The impulses in question are no longer solely the sexual impulses, but also the aggressive impulses. Because of the importance psychoanalysis has thenceforth attached to the defense of the ego and to aggression, its orientation is very different from the pansexual stereotype still held by the general public.

Present-Day Tendencies

Here Freud's own thought still dominates. Right up to his death in 1939 he continued to produce important works (such as, in 1926, *Inhibition, Symptom and Anxiety*). Psychoanalysis has continued to develop in England and the United States in an almost exuberant manner. It has lost ground in German-speaking countries, but important groups have been formed in Latin ones; in France the movement took shape from 1926 on.

Psychoanalysis has continued to develop in its technical, clinical, theoretical and applied aspects, especially in the extension of transformations of the Freudian doctrine, with a return to favor of some of the earlier concepts (like the notion of defense). Lack of therapeutic success, and theoretical difficulties, have led psychoanalysts to search for better solutions. We can discern three principal tendencies.

The first has involved an attempt to penetrate to deeper unconscious levels and to a past that lies even further back. Begun by Karl Abraham (1877–1925), this orientation is now represented by the British school and by Melanie Klein, who stresses the fundamental importance of the conflicts of earliest childhood. The later conflicts described by Freud— for example, castration anxiety and penis envy—are considered to provide explanations that, while not in themselves false, are relatively superficial.

By contrast, another school stresses the real conflicts of the individual with his environment. Karen Horney is a typical representative of this point of view. The "neurotic personality of our time" (the title of a 1937 work by her) is divided between its need for passive dependence and its defense against a hostile society. The therapist concentrates on the stratagems to which the ego has recourse in its confrontation with the world.

Along "Freudian" lines, the integrative function of the ego must be studied in its relation both to the external world and to the internal world of impulse. A typical representative here is Anna Freud, who stresses the similarity of the defense mechanisms employed by the ego as regards both external and internal stimulation. The ideal therapy starts from the wide area of the individual personality's relation both to the world and to itself, and retraces the whole neurotic process in order to reach the phantasies and decisive conflicts.

2 / *Psychoanalytic Perspectives*

To understand the works of psychoanalysis it is useful to know that in his study of "mental phenomena" Freud saw his subject from different points of view. According to him the most complete description is "metapsychological," because this gives us simultaneously a *dynamic,* an *economic* and a *structural* view of the situation.

From the dynamic point of view, psychoanalysis does not content itself with a description of mental phenomena, but explains them, through the interaction and opposition of forces; in other words, in terms of conflict. For example, an individual feels a surge of anger after experiencing humiliation, but restrains this, owing to a fear of counteraggression; this restraint alters the state of the organism and its relations with the environment. Briefly, the forces present in this conflict are impulses of biological origin (sexual and aggressive impulses) and counterimpulses of social origin.

The economic point of view stresses the quantitative aspect of the forces present in any conflict situation. For example, an individual may possess more or less powerful aggressiveness or sexuality from birth; this impulse energy is modified at certain critical stages of development (like puberty and the menopause). The relative strength of impulses and counterimpulses is decisive in the development of conflict. This energy may become displaced; to take the example of anger again, blocked aggression against a stronger adversary may escape in another situation with a less dangerous partner. Psychometric possibilities are limited in psychoanalysis, which is essentially a clinical discipline; however, they may be complemented by experiment on animals (measurement of drives, experimental studies of conflict, and so on).

The structure of the psychic apparatus is in question when we approach the problem from the topical or structural point of view. We have already seen that Freud substituted for the opposition of the preconscious and the unconscious a distinction of three systems—the id, the superego and the ego—which play their parts in different ways in conflict situations. These "aspects of the personality" can be distinguished both by their relative strength and by their origins.

A combination of the dynamic, economic and structural perspectives still does not give a sufficiently clear idea of what Freud meant by "metapsychology." The analogy of this term with "metaphysics" and "metapsychic" is misleading. The different works published under the label "metapsychology" have been extremely varied, and have covered such subjects as principles of mental functioning, repression, the unconscious, narcissism, transformation of impulses, and the theory of dreams and of melancholia. It is not possible to get an idea of metapsychology except by contrasting it with clinical psychoanalysis, which may be discovered in an ordered collection of case histories and their interpretation. As opposed to this, metapsychology becomes elaborated at a certain distance from actual facts, in the form of theoretical conceptualization, which reasons in terms of models and aims at causal explanation and the formulation of hypotheses in the general spirit of natural science. It is in fact a general psychoanalysis.

Freud included the genetic point of view with the dynamic. Hartmann and Kris (1946) have proposed making a distinction between the two. This point of view explains personality traits and modes of behavior in developmental terms. Freud early described stages in the development of impulses and relations with the object; an action, a trait, a symptom can always be characterized in terms of progression or regression. Analytic psychopathology has sought to link the neuroses and psychoses to predominant fixation points; for example, the obsessional neurosis to an anal-sadistic fixation, and depression to oral fixation.

Still another aspect has assumed growing importance in the last twenty-five years: that of *object relations*. This term denotes the various ways a subject is related to objects. And since objects are not only things but also people, object relations include the whole gamut of relations with others. Identification with others plays a major role in structuring the psychic apparatus. Thus current psychoanalytic views set "internalized" objects beside external objects and assign to them an important role.

3 / Fundamental Principles

Definition

By fundamental principles we mean the more general principles that govern mental life (according to the ideas of Freud), or put in another way, man's behavior and experience. These theoretical principles are constantly being applied in clinical practice and in technique. Historically, they arose when psychoanalysis itself came into being (1895). However, two periods must be distinguished. During the first, up to 1920, Freud tended to explain everything by the principle of pleasure-unpleasure; in the second, after 1920, he brought in "repetition compulsion" as acting "beyond the pleasure principle."

The Principle of Constancy

The principle of constancy—which has also been called the nirvana principle (Barbara Low)—is the tendency of the psychic apparatus to keep excitation at the lowest, or at least the most constant, level possible. This concept was borrowed by Freud from Fechner (1873), appears from the very beginnings of psychoanalysis (1895), and has never been abandoned. It takes into account simultaneously the processes of discharge that accompany satisfaction and those of defense against an excess of excitation.

The Principle of Pleasure-Unpleasure

More often called the "pleasure principle" for short, this is a consequence of the principle of constancy. All behavior originates in a state of painful excitation and tends to result in a reduction of this excitation, including the avoidance of pain, and whenever possible, the production of pleasure. The pleasure principle governs unconscious processes, left residually from a phase of development where they were the only mental processes, the primary ones. This is a state most nearly realized in the young child, at the age when he benefits from maternal care. He cheats the "unpleasure" arising from increases in stimulation and delays in satisfaction by crying and struggling, and by "hallucinating" the desired satisfaction. In the normally functioning adult the pleasure principle manifests itself in the shutting off of unpleasant impressions, and especially in dreams and daydreams. Sleep allows the recovery of a mental life comparable to the one that preceded the knowledge of reality, because sleep involves precisely such a rejection of reality. The ascendancy of the pleasure principle is greater in the neurotic: because reality is unendurable, he turns away from it, either completely or in part. Repression reflects a deficiency in "reality functioning," as Janet established.

The Reality Principle

By contrast, a corresponding progressive development is the increasing ascendancy of the reality principle, that is, of a modification of the pleasure principle that aims at the same goal, but through adjustment to conditions imposed by the external world. The reality principle does not dethrone the pleasure principle, but is only a safeguard. Immediate gratification is abandoned in favor of more certain ultimate satisfaction.

Insofar as the mental apparatus is concerned, the substitution of the reality principle for the pleasure principle is carried out through a development of conscious reality-adjustment functions (such as attention, memory and judgment) that substitutes action adequate for coping with reality for repression and simple motor discharge.

Thought possesses attributes that make it possible for the mental apparatus to endure increases in tension during the period when discharge must be postponed. It is essentially a method of experimental action accompanied by displacement and a lesser expenditure of energy, and it is likely that thought would not become conscious except for its connections with the memory traces for words. With the introduction of the reality principle, one method of mental activity becomes dissociated; imagination, as expressed in children's play and in daydreams, remains subordinate to the pleasure principle.

The progressive ascendancy of the reality principle is far from being uniform and general, and in large part impulses escape it. This is especially so with the sexual impulses, the maturation of which comes later: for a long time these are satisfied in an autoerotic manner, without becoming adjusted to real objects; and puberty is preceded by a long period of sexual latency. These conditions keep sexual impulses longer under the supremacy of the pleasure principle: they remain more closely bound to imagination, to "hallucinatory" satisfaction, to the repression that follows on the slightest painful impression. Therefore this is the weak point in mental organization, and it is understandable why the "choice of the neurosis" depends on the point at which ego and libido development become inhibited.

In general, unconscious processes remain under the control of the reality principle; thought becomes assimilated to reality, desire to its own realization. From which comes the danger of underestimating the transitory effect of phantasies, on the pretext that they correspond to nothing in reality; or of attaching a neurotic guilt feeling to some sort of tension, on the pretext that no crime has been committed in reality.

Freud connects the development of various cultural forms with the reality principle. Religions attempt to make men renounce pleasure in this life by the promise of recompense in the life to come. Science approaches most closely to a supplanting of the pleasure principle. Education tends to form the ego by replacing the pleasure principle by the reality principle. Art is a specific way of reconciling the two principles: the artist turns from the real to the imaginary, but he returns to reality and relies on the fact that the renunciation exacted by reality and painfully experienced by human beings is itself a part of reality.

Repetition Compulsion

The automatism of repetition (or better, repetition compulsion) is the tendency to repeat powerful experiences whatever their effects, favorable or harmful. From the beginning Freud recognized the importance of repetition processes, linking them with various concepts (fixation, regression and transference). But it was only after 1920 that he ascribed the importance of a principle of mental functioning to this compulsion, and said that it acted "beyond the pleasure principle." The psychological facts on which he based his argument were mostly taken from the traumatic neuroses, from children's play, from the neurosis of destiny (the repetition of the same troublesome life events), and from transference. Some of these repetitions can be reduced to the pleasure principle; for example, in a traumatic neurosis and in everyday life, repetition can serve the purpose of mastering a painful experience. However, a residue remains, and unhappy experiences, maladapted behavior, repeat themselves with tragic monotony. Since this repetition ends in frustration and in a wounding of self-esteem, we cannot interpret it as a repetition of needs seeking satisfaction. Rather, it arises from a specific need for repetition that transcends the pleasure principle. Certain biological views of a speculative nature amplify these psychological ideas. All life tends toward death, that is, toward a return to the inorganic, and sexuality tends toward reproduction. Thus repetition compulsion appears to be a psychological principle solidly anchored in biology.

Like the theory of the death instinct with which it is associated, the concept of repetition compulsion has met resistance and criticism. Basically, its critics seek to show that the repetition phenomena invoked in support of repetition compulsion are not "beyond the pleasure principle." The periodicity of impulses is rooted in their physical origins. Each time impulse demand asserts itself, guilt and ego defense must also come into force in a repetitive way. The large number of repetitions is explained by the persistence and recurrence of guilt feelings. And as for the repetitions of traumatic events, they involve essentially a search for a better answer, an attempt to master a situation not yet mastered. So an adult, when in a quandary over some quarrel, turns the matter over and over in his mind, searching for the perfect riposte with which to annihilate his adversary. When the effort at mastering fails while the need to master persists, a repetition of effort results (Kubie, Fenichel, Hendricks). Bibring, who is more conservative, distinguishes both a repetitive and a restitutive tendency in repetition compulsion. The repetitive tendency reflects the inertia of matter and is a preserving tendency, maintaining and repeating intense experiences, pleasant and painful alike; it is an impulse automatism situated beyond the pleasure principle. The restitutive tendency is a regulating mechanism charged with discharging tensions caused by traumatic experiences and so placing repetition in the service of the ego.

The striking thing about neurotic repetitions is the persistence of behavior inadequate for dealing with present reality, and the defeat of the reality principle, the powerlessness of symbolic thought, which alone could break the compulsive repetition by showing the effects of behavior in the future, through seeing things objectively. Repetition compulsion, on the contrary, expresses the dependence of the organism in relation to the needs and emotions it actually feels, and in relation to certain results of behavior felt to be imminent. In other words, actions described as compulsively repetitive are precisely characterized by primary, unconscious processes pertaining to the pleasure principle, in as much as this is distinguished from the reality principle. Such actions are the results of the ego's weakness and its powerlessness to disengage itself.

Links with Psychology

The four principles we have defined and discussed can be found in other forms in contemporary psychology. The Fechner-Freud principle of constancy is somewhat analogous to the physiologist Cannon's principle of homeostasis, and to the fundamental postulates of numerous behaviorists from Watson to Tolman. The reality principle takes into account secondary processes, or in psychological terms, learning processes: all the modifications of personality and behavior secondary to individual behavior and experience. The reality principle has been compared in particular with the "law of effect," according to which behavior is reinforced when it is "rewarded" and weakened when it is "punished." Repetition compulsion finds a parallel in the "principle of frequency," i.e. the connection between recall or recognition and the number of repetitions during the learning period. Problems that arise from the conflict of the pleasure principle and repetition compulsion have their corollary in psychological controversies over the principle of frequency and the law of effect. In both fields of research the persistence of repetitive and maladapted behavior is a key problem of psychology.

4 / Impulses

Definition

The idea of impulse has played a major part both in the
conceptualization of psychoanalytic discoveries and in the
systematization of the doctrine. The term was introduced
into the French translations of Freud as an equivalent for
the German *Trieb,* and also in order to avoid the implications of such older, non-psychoanalytic terms as "instinct"
and "drive."

This convention is far from being generally respected.
When Freud speaks of instinct, it is in the sense of animal
behavior determined by heredity and characteristic of the
species. When he speaks of impulse, it is in the sense of an
energetic motor "push" that inclines the organism toward a
goal. We can distinguish three points in the unfolding of the
impulse process: the *source,* which is a state of excitation
within the body; the *goal,* which is the suppression of this
excitation; and the *object,* which is the instrument by means
of which gratification is obtained.

The concept of impulse, therefore, lies between the

realms of the biological and the mental. It is less an observable reality than a "mythical" entity, the existence of which we are led to postulate behind the needs and activities of the organism. Classification of impulses depends on the criterion chosen; clinical experience has shown that the object and the goal are changeable, and physiology has no clear knowledge of the source. It is not surprising, then, that Freud's ideas on this subject evolved gradually.

The First Theory of the Impulses

Up to about 1920 the first theory of the impulses distinguished sexual impulses (designated in their dynamic manifestations by the term *libido*) and ego impulses. This theory was principally based on clinical experience of the part played by the repression of sexual needs in the pathogenesis of the neuroses. Anxiety, guilt and the moral or aesthetic ego ideals oppose sexual satisfaction. Forces opposed to the sexual tendencies and serving the preservation of the ego are therefore called *ego impulses*. Conflict between sexual impulses and ego impulses is thought to be the reason for neurotic conflict, and repression to be the result of dominant ego impulses.

Narcissism

One of the first modifications of the theory of the impulses came from the discovery between 1911 and 1914 of narcissism, i.e. of the libidinal or sexual nature of certain tendencies hitherto attributed to ego impulses. The thesis is that a certain part of egoism, or love of the self, is of the same nature as libido invested in external objects. Libido is the general energy of sexual impulses invested in the ego, in another person, or in things. The proof lies in the displacement of libido from the ego to objects, and vice versa. The sum of the interest invested in objects and in the ego is constant, so that the more one loves oneself, the less is one's love of objects, and vice versa. Thus in exhaustion, dreams, pain, ill health or sadness a greater or lesser part of the libido invested in external objects and other people reverts to the ego. Although capable of ultimately coming into conflict, the libido of the ego and "object" libido are similar and have the same origin. Thus the dialectical progress of Freud's thought united the impulses.

The Second Theory of the Impulses

This theory rests on the distinction between the life impulses and the death impulses. The impulses of life, or Eros, henceforth encompass opposition between preservation of self and preservation of species, in the same sort of unity as that of the narcissistic libido and the object libido; the goal is interconnection (in German, *Bindung*); that is, the goal is to establish ever-increasing, vaster totalities, and so to endure. The impulses of death and destruction, or Thanatos, have as their goal the disruption of connections, the ultimate goal of every living thing being a return to an inorganic state. Both the impulses of life and of death are conservative by nature, since both tend to re-establish a pre-existing state of affairs. This new dualism corresponds to the functions of the biological processes of construction and destruction in the living organism.

The projection of the self-destructive death impulse onto external objects produces destructive tendencies, whereas the life impulses, at first invested in the ego, produce object libido when projected. Behavior that is purely narcissistic or objective, destructive or libidinal, does not exist; all actions reflect either a conflict between or a combination of the two groups of instincts, and are either "fusions" or "integrations." Alterations in the mixture—"disintegrations of impulses"—result in behavior disorders; for example, excess of sexual aggression leads to love of murder, and excessive decrease in aggressiveness makes for timidity and impotence.

The hypothesis of the death impulses has met with resistance from many psychoanalysts. Its physical and biological foundations have been superseded. Destructive tendencies can be explained in other ways; aggression is the way in which certain goals are pursued at a primitive level, as a result of frustration, or spontaneously, through a lack of differentiation between aggression and libido. The principle of constancy furnishes us with a unique explanatory principle, whether the organism seeks a reduction in tension immediately, or attains it in a more roundabout way through higher tensions (an appetite for stimulation, exploration or the formation of greater totalities).

The Maturation of the Impulses

The source of an impulse is somatic and relatively independent of the interaction between the organism and the environment. Maturation of the body therefore determines maturation of impulses, through an internal development comparable to that of the embryo. This biological determination remains in force throughout life and manifests itself particularly during the periods of somatic transformation (childhood, puberty, menopause and senescence). The idea that the impulses have a chronological development by linked stages is an old one in psychoanalytic theory (1905); even though it has been modified, revised and enriched, it remains one of the most stable aspects of the theory. The key concept is that of *erogenous zones,* i.e. bodily regions the stimulation of which is a condition of libidinal satisfaction. The dominant erogenous zone changes with age and with the growth of the organism; this is called *impulse stages.* The organization of the rapport of the organism with itself, the environment and other people changes in a correlated manner; this we call *object stages.*

The primitive oral stage (sucking) corresponds to the first phase of life. The mouth is then the threshold for a dominant although not exclusive manner of approach, that of incorporation. This involves not only sucking at the maternal breast, but also the absorption by the sensory organs and skin of all stimuli entering the field accessible to the child. The more adequate the environment (and the mother in particular), the better the child's acceptance of what is offered. This is accompanied by an intense libidinal satisfaction, called *oral.* In the event. of frustration, tension or expectation, the child quickly learns to suck a part of its own body, most often its fingers, and especially the thumb, in this way attaining *autoerotic* satisfaction.

The later oral stage begins with the second phase of life. Incorporation by biting supersedes that by sucking: not only does the child take pleasure in biting, but its sensory and motor activities "bite" into reality; in relation to others, typical behavior consists of taking and keeping. Tension connected with teething makes the child gnaw at things all the more and poses him the problem of nursing without biting, to prevent the mother from removing the breast.

In addition there comes weaning. Conflict cannot be avoided however adequate the attitude of those around. Teething pains, anger with the mother, impotent rage involving the infant in confused sado-masochistic experiences: all leave the general impression that harmony with the mother has been destroyed. One calls the infant *ambivalent* since intimate union with an object implies its destruction. And since the infant is above all interested in his own body, he is said to be *narcissistic*.

The anal-sadistic stage extends over the second and third years of life. Tensions are mainly discharged through defecation. Libidinal satisfaction is connected with evacuations and the excitation of anal mucosa; excitation can be increased by retention. Fecal materials become ambivalent objects, since they can either be rejected or retained. They represent "possessions," since they are the issue of the body transformed into external objects. The association of sadism with anality is mostly due to the feeling that elimination is destructive, and to the fact that during toilet training, control over the sphincters becomes instrumental in opposing adults. The anal-sadistic stage is characterized by ambivalence and bisexuality.

The *phallic* stage falls between the third and fifth years. The genital organs (the penis with the boy, and the clitoris with the girl) become the dominant erogenous zones. Tensions are discharged by genital masturbation accompanied by phantasies. Tendencies that bring the child closer to members of the environment come to resemble more closely the love life of adults. With the boy, a positive Oedipus complex results from the fact that through an intensification of his love for his mother he feels conflict between his love for his father (based on his identification with the father) and his hate for his father (based on the father's privileges, which he is denied). Castration anxiety makes the boy renounce an exclusive right to possess the mother. (We speak of a negative Oedipus complex when the mother is experienced as interfering with love for the father.) With the girl, the development toward the father is more complex, and is prepared for by disappointments in the relationship with the mother, principally through lack of a penis; penis envy is replaced by the desire to have a child by the father.

Between the sixth year and puberty there is a *latency period* that corresponds to a decrease in impulse drive and is more determined by culture than by biological growth. The child forgets the "polymorphous perversity" of the preceding years (infantile amnesia) and develops morality in order to stem the onslaught of the impulses.

At puberty instinctual drives come into conflict with obstacles that did not exist during the development of infantile sexuality. The partial tendencies that characterized the latter (oral, anal and sado-masochistic tendencies, voyeurism, exhibitionism) do not disappear but become integrated and subordinate to genital primacy. In this way the *genital stage* becomes inaugurated; it is characterized by adult sexuality dominated by coitus.

If a person is prevented from fully realizing one of the instinctual stages of development, he can either make premature progress or regress to an earlier, more secure position, thus bringing about a *fixation* of impulse. Such a fixation results in a predisposition to the return of the stage's characteristic tendencies (for example, after some frustration). Such a return of the repressed plays a major role in the genesis of the neuroses and perversions (for example, the return of oral sadistic tendencies in the manic-depressive psychosis, or of anal-sadistic tendencies in the obsessional neurosis).

These are the main outlines of the classical conception (Freud, 1905; Karl Abraham, 1924). This conception has been criticized, enriched (Ruth Mack Brunswick, 1940) and modified by various authors (Melanie Klein). We shall confine ourselves to emphasizing that reality is more complex, that certain possibilities have been outlined, that others do exist and that in the last resort whether one set of possibilities or another is realized depends on the complex interaction of the child and his environment.

The Education of the Impulses

The idea of the impulses developing for themselves in a purely internal manner does not correspond to what happens in reality. Because of his biological immaturity the human child depends on his environment, and that environment tends to mold impulse development in conformity with its own demands. This action is conditioned by the plasticity of impulse objects and goals, the source of which alone remains a biological constant in the whole.

We can cite many examples of impulse transformation. Weaning gradually replaces the breast with the bottle and solid food (displacement). Toilet training implies a reversal of the attitude to the excretory functions (reaction formation) and an adherence to the mother's preferences (identification). The correction of an aggressive act by corporal punishment can turn sadism into masochism (reversal of an instinct into its opposite). A mechanism often called upon is *sublimation*; this simultaneously changes both the object and the goal of an impulse in such a way that the impulse can find its satisfaction in an object-goal that is no longer sexual but has a higher value, either socially or morally.

Thus in human behavior the impulses do not play the adaptive part that they do in many animals. Their orientation is alien to reality. Learning and socialization are necessary in human beings, and this passes on to the ego the function of preserving the organism and its adjustment to reality.

5 / The Personality

General Aspects

The concept of personality, which is so important in contemporary psychology, is even more important in psychoanalysis. As psychotherapy, psychoanalysis is a person-to-person relationship; and as psychology, it lays the greatest stress on personal history, and in this history, on interpersonal relationships. Because of this, psychoanalysts are not very concerned with giving a general definition of personality. Doubtless they do adapt a definition that will assimilate the personality, within the individual, to psychophysiological systems that assure its individual adjustment to the environment (Allport). On the other hand, psychoanalysis is one of the few forms of psychology that is preoccupied with the structure of the personality and the psychic apparatus.

The First Theory of the Psychic Apparatus

The first Freudian theory of the psychic apparatus is put forward at the end of *The Interpretation of Dreams*

(1900). Passing to the "topical" point of view, Freud elaborates a "fictitious" picture of a psychic apparatus responsible for the regulation of tension. The psychic apparatus is made up of two systems, the unconscious and the preconscious, between which the censor mediates (much as refraction occurs when light passes from one place to another).

The unconscious system is the stronghold of innate impulses and repressed desires and memories; ruled by the pleasure principle, "primary processes" are characterized by a mobile energy, which tends toward discharge and can easily become displaced or condensed upon objects and ideas, without regard for the rules of rational, objective thought (dreams).

The preconscious is the stronghold of mental operations known to psychology, of the capacity to learn and of the fruit of such learning. Latent but available, secondary processes are governed by the reality principle; the energy that characterizes them is "bound," and the characteristic operations are inhibition of impulses, postponement of discharge, and adjustment to reality. The passing of the unconscious into the preconscious is regulated by the censor: motivated by the conflict between tendencies acceptable to the person and repressed tendencies, its function is to fulfill or reject repression.

As for consciousness, it is a part of the free energy at the disposal of the preconscious; its role is to insure more discriminating adjustment. It can also, to a certain extent, resist the unpleasant tensions that motivate the censor's reaction. Freud conceived of psychic activity as essentially unconscious: unconscious desires lie at the heart of our being. All mental processes originate in the unconscious; finding access to the preconscious, they can either be repressed or become propagated, in the more or less disguised forms of affects, ideas, words or actions. The passing from the preconscious into consciousness is also controlled by the censor. In the last resort, consciousness alone can succeed in freeing mental processes, if only for a moment, from the ascendancy of the unconscious.

Between 1910 and 1920 Freud worked out the elements of an "ego" theory. The inadequacy of the first model became especially evident to him in the light of ego defense and the operations of repression. The first theory makes the unconscious coincident with the repressed matter. But reflection shows that in repression the working of repression is itself also unconscious. Thus the basic conflict can no longer be expressed in terms of a preconscious-conscious system, as against an unconscious system. The ego itself can be conscious, preconscious and also unconscious.

The Second Theory of the Psychic Apparatus

It was in *The Ego and the Id* (1923) that Freud first gave his second concept of the psychic apparatus. This concept consists in an isolation of three systems or aspects of the personality: the id, the ego and the superego.

These terms are sometimes used metaphorically by Freud himself. Clinical experience shows that the psychological realities to which they correspond can become projected, especially in dreams; for example, id impulses can be symbolized by an animal, or the forces of repression denoted by the superego can be projected in an image of a policeman. However, it is not useful to make entities or personages of these terms. They can only designate systems of motivation and action that are usually opposed in conflict.

The word *id* is a translation of *das Es*. The concept originated with Nietzsche and Groddeck, who meant by it all the impersonal, involuntary, unconscious and natural elements in the deep forces that govern human life. It is the original form of the psychic apparatus, such as exists in the prenatal period and in newborn babies—the primal matter from which later differentiation arises. Dynamically, it is composed of innate impulses (aggressive and sexual) and repressed desires. Its functioning is dominated by the primary process: the desires of the id are withdrawn from the reality principle, they disregard time, causal relations and logic, and they are subject to the pleasure principle. It is wrong to reduce the id to biological impulses, the impulses in question. If they succeed in becoming invested in real or symbolic objects, they concern, in the depths of the unconscious, objects and goals alien to reality, or properly speaking, "phantasy" objects.

THE ego (in German, *das Ich*) must not be confused with the ego of non-analytic psychology. According to Freud, the ego develops through differentiation in the psychic apparatus following contact with external realities, just as the id becomes differentiated following contact with the somatic sources of needs and emotions. The activity of the ego is conscious (perception, external and internal, intellectual processes), preconscious and unconscious (defense mechanisms). Ego structure is dominated by the reality principle (objective, socialized, rational and verbal thought). It is the ego, and not the id or the impulses, that undertakes the defense of the individual and his adjustment to his environment, and the solution of conflicts with reality or between incompatible desires; it controls access to consciousness and action and insures the "synthetic function of the personality." The ego also defines the person himself, insofar as he is the object of perceptions, attitudes and affects; for example, in narcissism, in which the individual is the object of his own love (Nunberg).

THE superego (in German, *das Überich*) is, in the classical conception, a modification of the ego by the internalization of the repressive forces the individual has encountered during the course of his development. Its activity becomes manifest in the case of conflict with the ego by the development of emotions connected with moral consciousness—principally guilt. Attitudes of self-observation, self-criticism and prohibition, which exist normally, take such exaggerated forms in certain neuroses (obsession, melancholia) that extreme anxiety makes life intolerable; in such states of "moral masochism" the individual is dominated by an irresistible need for self-accusation and punishment, suffering and failure.

The superego is formed by the child's identification with idealized parents, normally with the parent of the same sex. Freud assigned the major role to the identifications that resolve the Oedipal conflict, but more precocious identifications and later ones are also included. If the superego does not become completely depersonalized, it retains a prerational, anthropomorphic structure; everything continues as if an archaic relation—real, imaginary or symbolic —were still in existence between a strict father and his child. The profound affinity between the superego and the id results from the superego's being the end product of the child's identification with the first objects of his sexual and aggressive impulses. Both represent past influence—the id that of heredity, the superego that of parental and social influences—whereas the ego is mainly determined by the individual's own experience. These are reasons for thinking that the superego can in fact exist before the individual himself comes into being.

The ego ideal corresponds to what the individual must be to fulfill the requirements of the superego. The ideal ego (with which the ego is often confused) corresponds to what a person expects of himself in order to fulfill the requirements of an infantile illusion of omnipotence, of a primary identification with an all-powerful parent.

To sum up, the ego directs and controls the person's adjustment to the environment, the tensions that motivate him and the realization of his potentialities. The ego is limited in its action not only by the absence or inadequacy of certain aptitudes, but also by infiltrations from the id and the superego that force it to act in the wrong way or prevent it from acting; examples are repetition compulsion and moral masochism.

The Genesis of the Personality

Thus a psychoanalytic cure involves the relations of the three aspects of the psychic apparatus in the subject as these come to grips with external reality (Anna Freud,

1936). By comparing individual histories we can extract a description of the genetic stages, the outcome of which is the structure and the dynamics of the personality. Analytic personology attributes decisive importance to the first five years of life, and indeed to the first two or three.

This formation has always been conceived as resulting from an interaction between biological and psychosociological determinants, and especially from the family environment, which is the agent for the concrete and particular transmission of culture. In the earlier systematizations biological tendencies predominate. Stages in object relations correspond to stages in the maturation of the instincts; the significance and import of external events are bound to the impulse stage in which they occur. The directions the emotions take and the child's phantasies are largely regulated by the maturation of impulses. According to Freud, the origin of the Oedipus complex is partly explicable in terms of a collective unconscious (to which Jung has attached greater importance). Today such explanations seem too simple: impulse development seems less schematic, impulse stages may perhaps be only cultural artifacts, and the latency period is no longer considered to be universal. The hypothesis of a collective unconscious seems a costly one; we are more struck by the universal biological prematurity of the child, which makes it dependent on its environment for a long time. We have become more conscious of the complexity of the interaction between biological maturation and environment; and psychoanalysis has thrown open its doors to the methods and contributions of other disciplines (direct observation of children as individuals or in groups, cultural anthropology). In recent decades research has concentrated on the first three years, on the mother-child relationship, and on precocious forms of the ego and super-ego.

It is impossible to give an idea here of these difficult and controversial questions (of which Gerald Blum has made an inventory). On the whole, the formation of the personality seems to involve a progressive socialization in the development of which many successive identifications play a part—a point clarified by psychoanalysis. One of the effects of identification is to remedy fragmentation of the child's experience of its environment and of its own body, although failure to coincide exactly with another person works against this.

6 / Behavior

General Aspects

We cannot define the object of psychoanalytic research as conscious experience—since psychoanalysis seeks to detect unconscious meanings—nor as unconscious processes—since psychoanalysis has evolved toward the totality of the subject's rapport both with his environment and with himself. The concept of behavior, which implies nothing as regards the conscious or unconscious quality of mental processes, is the one that best allows a regrouping of the theoretical notions of the preceding chapters around the phenomena provided by clinical experience.

Behavior is not defined here as purely external, material manifestations. Rather it is the totality of the physiological, mental, verbal and motor actions by which a person involved with his environment tries to resolve the tensions that motivate him and to realize his potentialities. Its essential character is to have a meaning, which is the property through which the actions that comprise it are articulated one with another, and so reduce motivating tensions. It includes conscious experience, a symbolic way of behaving that substitutes for material action or prefaces it. It includes communication, an essential aspect of the subject's explanation of his environment.

Motivation

Motivation is a state of dissociation and tension that puts the organism into action until it has reduced the tension and recovered its harmony (the principle of constancy). We have already seen that for psychoanalysis the ultimate source of motivation is impulse, modeled on personal experience and socialization. Motivation manifests itself through two main forms, the needs and the emotions.

Needs are extremely varied in both strength and nature; they include physiological needs and the needs for security, love, esteem, knowledge and understanding, suffering and punishment, and so on. They are concrete manifestations of the impulses but are more plastic, since their satisfaction is less imperious and indispensable to the organism's survival; for example, the sexual needs and the need for freedom are far more plastic than the need to breathe. The emergence of needs is accompanied by a feeling-tone that is pleasant or painful, according to whether the ego anticipates frustration or satisfaction. The term *desire* belongs more particularly to a need that is connected with a goal and with an object relevant to attaining this goal. *Demand* denotes the insertion of desire into the relationship with another.

Aversion is opposed to desire. Psychoanalysis has connected this especially with painful emotions, which are closely bound up with important needs. Typical is anxiety or anguish, which is bound up with the need for security. In its primitive form aversion is mingled with every state of tension or excessive stimulation, which precludes the possibility of adequate response in the organism (a traumatic state). Secondarily, aversion becomes weakened or transformed into a danger signal serving ego defense. If defense measures fail, the ego is overwhelmed and experiences panic. Guilt and anxiety prevail when the subject does not respond to the expectations of the superego, which represents inner moral authority. Like anxiety and guilt, other painful emotions (such as distaste and shame) together constitute *defense motives;* these put the defensive activity of the ego into operation.

The Elaboration of Behavior

The elaboration of behavior consists in the conscious awareness of the subject's needs, and in the discovery of goals, objects and means appropriate for their satisfaction. Resolution of tension, realization of potentialities, and adjustment to reality are therefore the functions of the ego. Hence the importance of everything that decreases the action of the ego, such as excessive impulse strength (i.e. excessive needs and emotions), repetition compulsion (which impedes a thoughtful adjustment to distant effects) and guilt and moral masochism. In topographical terms, ego strength corresponds to the ego's degree of freedom in relation to the two other aspects, the id and the superego.

Research on Methods

This point in behavior has been explored by psychology under such categories as habit, exploration and intelligence. But for a long time psychoanalysis was not interested in these processes, leaving the ego to be studied by psychologists. However, this study has taken on great importance in the last thirty years, and important works have been dedicated to these problems (by Hartmann and Rapaport, among others). Freud himself produced a basic formulation for a modern theory of thought, describing it as a mental experiment in which the postponement of response and the anticipation of effects play a major role. An important aspect of ego weakness is that the ego cannot bring symbolic thoughts into play, owing to its inability to withdraw from the immediate constraints of environment, emotions and desires.

Objects

To become discharged a need must find an adequate object. This object may be external (alloplastic behavior) or it may be the person himself (autoplastic behavior), as when the response is confined to an emotion, to defense by repression, or to an autoerotic satisfaction. The choice of an object is plastic, like the impulse goal; as a result, the choice of an object adequate to the need or of substitute objects that are also satisfying (as in sublimation) falls upon the ego. This is always provided that the ego's freedom of action is not impeded by fixation to a past internalized object. For example, a satisfying choice of a lover is made difficult for a man if he is fixated on an ambivalent mother who was sometimes gratifying and sometimes frustrating, so that he had recurrently to reconquer her love when he believed he had lost it. In such a case fixation on a certain kind of object is closely linked to fixation on certain goals. Interference from unconscious object fixations manifests itself in distorted perception of real objects, upon which the *imago* of good and bad objects, of idealized and persecuting objects, is projected.

Discharge and Defense

The general goal of behavior is the reduction of tension and dissociation, i.e. integration. As a result of the plasticity of impulse goals, the ego plays a major part in the determination of goals, while taking into account both external and internal reality. Here ego efficiency is impaired by fixation on certain unconscious goals, for example, that of moral masochism, a need to suffer and to punish oneself that poisons the existence of so many human beings, not only the masochists but also their associates. Two eventualities may be distinguished. Either behavior leads to a satisfying discharge, through an increase in tension and the experience of pleasant emotions (for example, in normal sexual intercourse that ends in orgasm); or the emergence of a desire is accompanied by a sense of danger; its development is impeded by interference from painful emotions (distaste, shame and especially anxiety and guilt). In an automatic and unconscious manner the ego brings its defense mechanisms into action, both against the painful emotions and against the desires that have motivated them; the goal of behavior is always the reduction of tension, but without an increase in intermediary tension in rejecting and dissociating from the ego painful emotions and censorable desires. This is a costly process of adjustment because it must be continued or repeated, and because the repressed impulse continues to exist in its derivative form, erupting into behavior and conscious experience in roundabout ways without being recognized by the ego.

Defense mechanisms have been studied by Anna Freud (1936) and by Fenichel (1944). The general effect of these mechanisms is *repression* into the unconscious. This term also denotes a special defense mechanism; an unconscious tendency not to make conscious, or to forget, tendencies or events that usually represent temptations, punishments or allusions to unacceptable desires; for example, certain intentions or a name are forgotten, or the context and meaning of an emotion. Other defense mechanisms have been described: denial, or the tendency to deny painful facts and impressions; reaction formation, such as cleanliness and love of order deriving from the struggle against dirt and disorder; retroactive undoing, which consists in doing something that, either in reality or magically, is the opposite of something that has been done either in reality or in imagination. Ego defense also comes into force against painful emotions, or rather against the tensions that the ego prevents from developing in painful emotions; for example, the postponement of an emotion in a critical situation. Defenses against emotions are the same as against impulses; repressed emotions, like repressed impulses, remain active and manifest themselves indirectly (in dreams, symptoms, substitutes and somatic equivalents).

Among the ego defense mechanisms it is convenient to distinguish those concerned with ego disengagement from a quite different adaptive value, the effectiveness of which depends on a lifting of the defense; for example, the labor of becoming detached from a loved one during mourning. We place here sublimation, which differs from the other defense mechanisms in that its discharge is not blocked. Examples include the sublimation of homosexual impulses in friendship and social relations; the sublimation of sadistic impulses in the surgeon; and the sublimation of oral impulses in the singer and the orator.

The Secondary Effects of Behavior

The effects of behavior are not confined to the reactions of discharge or defense that have been defined as their goals. Behavior also has secondary effects. One of these is the formation of the personality and of a whole system of habits. But in addition behavior has secondary effects, external to the personality; it induces reciprocal reactions in other people, and the repetition of certain kinds of behavior can thus result in an incredibly similar repetition of events.

A young woman often found herself making a third in some relationship; for instance, being both the wife's friend and having the husband pay her attentions and show her love. At an interval of several months, with two different couples, the wife called on her to wake up the husband, who had trouble waking up, before setting off on a journey.

This almost identical repetition of events in themselves unfavorable (men deceived by their mistresses or betrayed by their best friends) Freud called *neurosis of destiny.*

Consciousness and Unconsciousness

In its early stages psychoanalysis concentrated on the unconscious and tended to underestimate the conscious, reducing it to a by-product of the unconscious processes that constitute psychic reality. Freud's writings on the role of consciousness and the reality principle show that he him-self never committed this excess. The development of ego psychoanalysis has made conscious activities better under-stood; besides, a grasp of unconscious processes has always played a major part in pychoanalytic cures. It is the same as in the case of the conflict with defense mechanisms, where repressed desires and emotions exercise an unper-ceived pressure on the ego; from this comes distortion in perceiving other people and situations (projection), and also the tendentious justification of actions really motivated by the unconscious (rationalization). The "alienated" ego finds justifications for itself, just as does the subject who awakens from the hypnotic trance and needs a reason for carrying out an order he has received when hypnotized.

Behavior and Communication

Communication concerns at least two people, the au-thor of the message and the addressee, whose roles alter-nate. Communications can make use of all sorts of media, but what matters is its goal—i.e. the transmission of the meaningful—and its effects are at once alloplastic and symbolic. Some social behavior is essentially a form of com-munication; as for the rest, few actions are not in some respect communication. The most familiar example of com-munication is the word. The reciprocal play of expression and comprehension, and their continuous adjustment, pre-suppose mental experiences of partial identification; to com-municate is to share. This is well demonstrated by diffi-culties in communication, which produce heterogeneity of the conscience experience. Communication requires that the people involved be distinct (without which it would be useless) and that in some ways they be similar (without which it would be impossible).

The problem of communication is crucial for psychopathology and psychoanalysis. The whole process of cure can be described as a transition from inadequate to adequate communication; psychoanalyst and psychoanalysand have to resolve misunderstandings (Ferenczi, 1927). Communication is hindered, for example, by the projection that transforms the psychoanalyst into a judge and the patient's "free associations" into the forced confession of a guilty child to a strict parent.

Communication does not make use of language alone, and the patient's every action is hypothetically a communication, which may reveal what words conceal. Different problems are posed by the existence of messages whose material transmission it is not always possible to grasp.

Instead of isolating the organism, modern psychology is centered on the interactions of the organism with the subject's environment and with others. Consciousness is described, not as closed, but as open to the world. The same movement in psychoanalysis has produced the concept of object relations. The basis of interpersonal relations is communication.

7 / Everyday Life

Psychoanalysis and Everyday Life

The evocation of everyday life makes us think of Freud's work on psychopathology. It holds psychoanalysis back. During the course of treatment, what is happening in the current life of the patient makes its appearance again and again, often to the extent of getting in the way of a cure through the intensity and urgency of conflicts. Psychoanalytic literature has data on these subjects. Works exist on all aspects of daily life, although the psychoanalytic production bears more on psychopathology as such. All the fields and activities in which man takes part are accessible to psychoanalysis, provided we proceed through adequate investigation.

Psychoanalysis does not pretend to give exhaustive explanations. It does not despise biological, social, economic and cultural determinants; for example, it is plain that much behavior expresses social usages. The scope of psychoanalysis covers the behavior and experience of individuals, and their interpersonal relations; its specific goal is to isolate the meaning of this totality and its consequences. So, despite a mass of data and some interesting studies, the psychology of marriage has yet to be formulated: vast statistical inquiries and advanced clinical studies do not allow subtle and deep analysis, so that it is necessary to turn to psychoanalysis if we want complete understanding of the choice of partners and the development of conjugal ties and conflicts.

Thus daily life provides psychoanalysis with numerous fields of research. There is no activity where unconscious desires and objects do not intrude—which does not mean that everything must be reduced to unconscious processes. We can easily demonstrate the part played by projection in the perception of other people and situations, and the part played by rationalization in "voluntary" activity. We have already seen the part people can play in shaping the events of their life (the neurosis of destiny). An important mechanism is that of "acting out"—very highly developed in some people, who seem to devote an unconscious ingenuity to the business of actualizing and dramatizing in their current lives themes from their unconscious dramas, with the aim of satisfying certain desires or mastering traumatic situations.

Certain forms of failure are cases in point. Stereotyped repetition of the same situations and the same complaints shows that the person involves himself in this way for a reason. The psychological sequence is often as follows: Through his attacks or clumsiness the person turns others against him, and a state of affairs results in which he can see himself as an innocent victim quite justified in blaming bad luck or the unkindness of human beings. Repetition compulsion produces an interplay of unconscious aggres-

sive desires and self-punishment, and perpetuates a persecuting relationship with others.

Slips and Errors

We can observe this phenomenon in ourselves, and can
often understand it. Freud lists here slips in speech and
writing, reading or hearing something wrong, momentary
forgetting of proper names and intentions, temporary losses
of different things, and momentary errors. He does not deny
the part played here by the reasons usually given, such as
fatigue, excitement, distractedness, or the linguistic char-
acteristics of words. But such explanations give only half
the answer. Psychoanalysis demonstrates that this disturbance in ego activity is connected with a parasitical motivation, often either conscious or preconscious and easily rec-
ognizable by the subject, or in other cases unconscious and
rejected by the ego.

Freud tells the story of the chairman of a meeting who,
not expecting any good result from it, opened it by declar-
ing it closed. Again, a patient whom Freud had forbidden
to telephone his mistress "by accident" always asked for his
mistress' number when wanting to speak to Freud himself.
A young man who wanted to take the arm of a young woman
who had a bad leg said: "Would you like me to take you in
my arms?" A girl who wanted to express the idea that it was
her mother who played the masculine role in the family
said "my father" when she meant "my mother."

The interpretation of such slips and errors enters into
the current practice of psychoanalysis. Their structure is
often quite simple, as when a subject expresses a positive

desire to die when he had intended to deny this. Their theoretical interest lies in showing by easily accessible examples the characteristic of psychoanalytic explanation, which is to unravel the meaning of actions seen in their totality and with their attendant consequences, while allowing due importance to other, partial determinants.

8 / Sleep, Dreams and Nightmares

Sleep and Insomnia

Sleep is a way of behaving by which the organism satisfies its need for rest, or more specifically, for sleep. Peaceful slumber without dreams corresponds to the most complete reduction of tension a living organism can normally attain. The sleeper wishes to know nothing more about reality. And so sleep produces a state in which the ego is relatively weak and motivations arising from the id and the superego are relatively reinforced. Genetically, Freud interpreted it as a return to prenatal existence: "We create conditions for ourselves that are at least analogous to those of that existence— warmth, darkness, lack of stimulation. Some of us roll up tight and make the body seem, during sleep, as if it were within the mother's body."

Sleep, then, implies a dominance of the desire to sleep and a weakening of other desires. Therefore disturbances of sleep, sleep that is not very restful or lack of sleep are the result of the emergence of disturbing tensions. The mechanism of certain types of insomnia is obvious, as when sleep is troubled by external stimulations, or by sharp, conscious cares, expectation charged with painful or pleasant emotions, unsatisfied sexual excitation or repressed anger. In the less obvious cases, the disturbance originates in repressed desires and emotions, often the association of temptation with fear of punishment; for example, a fear of masturbation and pollution, or of killing or being killed. The temporary enfeeblement of the ego can itself be feared, in the sense that it makes the sleeper less able to defend himself against the unacceptable impulses and that it can itself be interpreted as a punishment. In other people, by contrast, sleep is used as a defense against a reality that is not very satisfying, or against painful tensions.

The Dream

In dreaming, the ego, which wants to sleep, tries to reduce the motivations that tend to awaken the sleeper. Hence Freud's two famous sayings: "The dream is the guardian of sleep"; and "The dream is the fulfillment of a wish." In a more complex way, dreaming is not essentially different from transitory mistakes or forgetfulness.

Freudian formulae fit the case in its simplest form when the disturbing tendency develops without any check from reality or the ego. This is so when the ego and the sense of reality are not strongly developed, as in children. Let us recall one of Freud's examples:

A boy of twenty-two months was entrusted with presenting someone with a basket of cherries on an anniversary. He obviously did this with extreme reluctance, even though he had been promised some cherries for himself as a reward. Next day he described a dream he had in which "He(r)mann ate all the cherries."

Such infantile-type dreams recur in adults, especially under pressure from imperious physiological needs (hunger, thirst and sexual or toilet needs).

Ordinarily things are not so simple: the dream seems to have no sense, and its emotional tone is enigmatic or neutral; the sleeper says his dream was absurd, bizarre or curious. This is because dream thought does not have the same structure as waking thought. The manifest content is an abridgement of the latent content (condensation); each manifest element depends on several latent thoughts (overdetermination); the emotional stress becomes detached from its true object onto some accessory object (displacement); conceptual thought is expressed in visual representation (dramatization); either universal symbols are used or those of cultural or individual origin (symbolization); and finally, the sleeper's ego introduces a logical order or a tendentious interpretation into the dream material, as the sleeper approaches waking thought (secondary elaboration). These mechanisms (of which the first three characterize the "primary process") not only have descriptive significance, but possess a function. In the infantile-type dream satisfaction can be experienced without disguise because it does not arouse ego objection; but if the dream-disturbing desire or affect is of the kind to arouse conflict with the ego, the dream cannot carry out its function of guarding sleep unless its meaning is sufficiently masked.

The mechanisms through which the dream is elaborated allow a compromise between the demands of the ego and repressed motivation. Often the activity of ego defense appears most clearly in the manifest content; to this activity Freud gave the name *censor,* in his *Interpretation of Dreams.*

For example: A young married woman dreams she is in a flat occupied by Americans. She is shown a photograph album, chooses a partner for a dance, and is given a ticket. She understands that something else is in question but quiets her scruples. The man she has chosen is gentleman enough not to exact more than she can concede. She goes as a journalist to discover the facts. Here the dream grows more confused. She takes flight. Someone shoots at her in the dark. She escapes, however, and jumps onto a passing bus.

This dream dramatizes a wish to be unfaithful. The development of ego defense is easy to follow. The choice of a partner for a dance disguises the choice of a lover. The dreaming woman understands this so well that she has to defeat her guilt feelings by rationalizations: the man of her choice will demand nothing she cannot give, and she is to go as a journalist to get information. These defense measures fail. The ego then resorts to confusion, to forgetting part of the dream, and to flight. But the conflict between sexuality and guilt becomes more acute. The shot in the dark is a compromise, at once a symbol of a sexual attack and of punishment. At the same time the jump aboard the bus reconciles flight and sexual relations, so often symbolized by traveling on some sort of vehicle.

However transparent a dream may be, and whatever the psychoanalyst's intuition and experience, dreams require interpretation. In *The Interpretation of Dreams* Freud recommended investigating the dreamer's association of ideas in connection with various dream fragments, since such fragmentation has the aim of eliminating the apparent meaning and the secondary elaboration. As far as we know, this technique is no longer used: the psychoanalyst confines himself more or less, in provoking association of ideas, to certain points in the dream. The structure and secondary elaboration of the dream—its spontaneous interpretation by the dreamer—are used to indicate the defensive activity of the ego; as, for example, when an analysand gives the meaning of masochistic submissiveness to an all-powerful analyst to a dream of aggression directed against the analyst.

In general, the analyst tries to grasp the meaning of the dream within the current of the analysis by placing it in its context—by situating it in relation to various systems of reference presented by the psychoanalytic situation, current life, the physical state, the past and childhood. Dream interpretation is subordinated to the general conduct of the analysis. Often the analysis of a dream is not completed without new problems appearing; and conversely, parts of a dream that remain obscure may be illuminated in the course of the analysis.

One of the most original contributions to the psychoanalysis of dreams has been that of Bertram D. Lewin. To Lewin, sleep is a return to an oral nurturance satisfaction that slumbers when it has been satiated. The *dream screen* represents the maternal breast and the achievement of the desire to sleep. Parasitical desires, which may be either preconscious or conscious, and which threaten to waken the sleeper, form the visual content of the dream and realize other desires than that of staying asleep.

The Painful Dream and the Nightmare

The formula "the dream is the fulfillment of a wish" cannot be taken literally except in the case of "infantile" dreams. The wish the dream fulfills is the ego's desire to sleep. The dream does not develop and does not completely accomplish its function as guardian of sleep unless the activity of ego defense succeeds. In the opposite event, the dream takes on an anxious tone or is interrupted by an anxious awakening, as with the night fears of children.

There are dreams in which the manifest content appears obviously to contradict the fulfillment of a desire; such are the dreams in which the dreamer submits to painful treatment, for instance, to a judgment or a condemnation to death. The explanation is usually simple: the dominant need freed by the dream is a need for punishment (moral masochism), and so the punishment can occur after the offense or even before.

For example, here is part of the dream of a young man of twenty whose adolescent crisis was protracted and ended in a serious obsessional neurosis:

> We were playing with some friends of about the same age. My sister and I went up to my father and twisted his wrists in revenge. The people present were ashamed to attack an elderly man and disapproved of our behavior. The idea occurred to me to say I was sorry. I don't know what punishment my sister had, perhaps a slap or two from my father. But I fell on my knees to beg his pardon. My father first struck me lightly, then more and more heavily,

and finally punched me violently on the face. This hurt me as if I were really being hit. And then I felt an upsurge of anger. . . .

The key to the dream was sexual guilt shared with the sister and, in the past, sanctioned by the parents; the father's authority had remained an obstacle to sexual freedom. Thus the dream satisfied both a desire for vengeance and one for revolt against the father, who inspired an intense feeling of guilt and a need for expiation: "It was I who asked for punishment, because it was something so bad. My father didn't want to hit me and it got harder because I asked for it myself." Once the punishment was over a feeling of anger with the father was experienced. Besides this, the interdiction against incest and all sexuality led to homosexual passivity in relation to the father; in this sense the dream revealed both moral masochism and erogenous masochism, the source of a neurotic pleasure that could not be experienced except as unpleasant because it was unacceptable to the ego.

There is one dream category, however, that it seems impossible to reduce to the fulfillment of an infantile wish. This consists in the dreams of the traumatic neurosis, in which the dreamer sees again and again, in a stereotyped way, the traumatic event that determined his illness. According to Freud, these dreams obey the automatism of repetition, which aims at "evoking an anxiety state in the patient, which may allow him to escape from the ascendancy of the excitation he has undergone, an anxiety the absence of which caused traumatic neurosis." This function of the psychic apparatus is not opposed to the pleasure principle but is more primitive. The tendency of the dream to fulfill a desire is a later product.

Fenichel describes the same idea more accessibly. The archaic ego repeats actively what it has experienced passively, before being able to repeat something mentally or to anticipate (anxiety); the dream of traumatic repetition is a regression to this primitive way of mastery. It brings about a delayed discharge; also, it makes sleep possible despite inner tension.

Sometimes the traumatic dream conforms to a repressed desire. That is, the trauma has already conformed to this desire and its traumatic quality is bound up with this conformity, because the desire cannot be fulfilled without clashing violently with the ego defense.

For example, a war widow of forty-four was in a state of pathological mourning, which began a few days after the death of her only son, who was killed in a car accident. During the day she relived the drama: his departure, the emergency ward, her son in his coffin. At night she could not sleep but was in anguish through feeling her son's presence. If she fell asleep she was awakened by repetitive nightmares in which she saw her son dead again, stretched out on a table in the emergency ward, his head bandaged.

After a few sessions sleep improved and dreams took the place of nightmares.

In one of the first dreams, her son was a little boy; she was combing his hair and noticed some lice on his head, which astonished her. She remembered a neighbor's child to whom this "accident" happened. Her son had died in an accident from a fracture of the skull. On the evening of his death she had refused to give him some money and had reproached him for spending too much; she had been overcritical and "searched for lice."[1] She reproached herself for having "only themes such as these in her head" (identification). She also called up her ambivalence for her brother, her junior by eighteen years, whose birth she had taken badly.

Her ambivalence toward her well-loved son appeared more clearly in a second dream: "I have in my arms an infant all in swaddling bands except for his feet; the child gets on my nerves and I put him down on a couch with a cushion under his head."

She brought out various memories relating to her brother's birth. A woman cousin who was present in the dream had told her the news, and she had not welcomed it. In the dream it was as if she had another brother. Before her son's death she had often had dreams in which she was holding in her arms infants who embarrassed her; her son had prevented her from remarrying or having a liaison. Allusions to the accident follow from the cushion that she put under the infant's head and from the fact that the infant seemed to be mummified (she put into effect actively something she had previously submitted to passively). Over and over again she complained of being tormented by her son, who stood beside her and tortured her while she wished she was elsewhere.

This dream makes it possible to reconstruct the patient's situation before the accident, which was connected

---

[1] In French, "to be overcritical" can be expressed as "to search for the little animals" on someone.

with a long-standing ambivalence motivated by the late birth of her young brother—an obstacle to love and freedom.

This ambivalence reinforced her ambivalence toward her son—an obstacle to sexual freedom. So the patient had loved her son all the more, not only because of a concentration of libido, but because she had to compensate for and repress an unconscious hostility. Thus her son's death not only represented the loss of her principal love object but was also the brutal gratification of a deeply repressed hostility. The repetition of the drama in the nightmares did not just represent the overwhelming of the ego and its recourse to an archaic way of mastering the situation through active repetition; it also protected her against repressed hostility toward her son, a hostility it was necessary to keep repressed in order that the work of mourning and libidinal detachment might be accomplished.

The difficulties arising from the formula "the dream is the fulfillment of a wish" (and from making wishes date from childhood) disappear when we keep in mind that the desire the dream guarantees to satisfy is the ego's desire to sleep. The dream is an attempt to reduce tension, an excessive degree of which produces anxiety, nightmares and sleeplessness.

9 / Psychic Disorders

The Functional Conception of Behavioral Disorders

By the end of the nineteenth century mental pathology was well launched. Many unknown factors remained, but psychiatrists had accumulated a great store of information on the clinical forms, development and causes of mental illnesses. Diagnosis was oriented toward the identification of different illnesses. Causal explanations, stimulated by the discoveries of the anatomical-clinical method, drew mainly on hereditary constitution, lesions or somatic disorders, whether real or hypothetical. Life events were considered to play only an incidental part.

Psychoanalysis has brought few changes into psychiatric nosography (the description of types of disease). The essential characteristic of the psychoanalytic attitude is the effort to grasp the meaning of the clinical picture as a whole, insofar as it expresses the patient's relations with the world and with himself and represents the developmental force of the personality. In other words, the originality of psychoanalysis lies in its introduction of a functional concept of mental illness. Mental illness is an attempt at adjustment, an effort to solve problems that cannot be solved more satisfactorily.

Conflict is a common factor in health and sickness. Conflict is not in itself pathological. For both physiologist and psychologist, life is an alternation of equilibrium and disequilibrium, a succession of attempts and errors in reestablishing equilibrium once it has been lost. When these efforts succeed, when this adjustment produces a better equilibrium between the organism and the environment, simultaneously with a complete fulfillment of the living being's potentialities, we are right in speaking of a normative or constructive integration. In other cases the organism does not succeed in resolving the conflict, and the characteristic tension and dissociation persists. Or the organism elaborates inadequate solutions that only decrease painful tension as they increase dissociation, by bringing into play those "dissociative adjustments" discovered by psychoanalysis. In these last two resorts conflict is not resolved but becomes perpetual. In becoming the "norm" it becomes "anormal." But behavioral disorder, although objectively ineffective and subjectively painful, does constitute a kind of order. The organism modifies itself by reducing the most powerful, immediate or painful tensions. The orientation of conflict toward integrative or dissociative adjustments, i.e. health or sickness, is, however, mysterious from many points of view. Psychoanalysis conforms to biological tradition in admitting the fundamental role of somatic conditions (heredity, age and maturation, physiopathological processes), but stresses the role of individual experiences (situations, events, traumata, family and social factors), or briefly, of "learning" as it is now called, as opposed to "maturation." All the same, the significance and efficacy of learning factors are very dependent on maturation. The meaning and import of an event depend on the developmental stage at which it occurs. Sometimes the weight of biological factors is such that quite slight external obstacles are enough to disturb development; at other times the biological foundation is so good that the human being can extricate himself from the worst situations. In general, the quantitative (economic) factors are decisive; for example, the strength of external and internal stimulation, and the state of development and strength of the ego. But at the point of departure we cannot yet disclose the decisive differences between the man who is going to be ill and the one who will be well. Differentiation is only possible after the fact, since illness brings out potentialities that remain latent or are much less noticeable and disturbing, in the individual who is well. In this way homosexuality, which in our society is a marked anomaly of sexual and social adaptation, can be uniformly discovered in all sexually well-adapted adults as an underlying possibility.

Psychoneuroses

The special interest of the psychoneuroses lies mainly in two facts: the first psychoanalytic discoveries were made in connection with them; and they are the most suitable for psychoanalytic treatment. They are the *transference neuroses;* that is, those in which unconscious neurotic conflict can best be introduced into the relation between the patient and the analyst.

From a descriptive viewpoint, negative and positive

symptoms may be distinguished. The patient is more or less hampered in carrying out actions that have as their goal the satisfaction of the personality, the realization of potentialities, and adjustment to reality. For example, the patient complains of insomnia, inability to concentrate, or sexual inhibition, such as impotence or frigidity. Positive symptoms seem to originate from an unknown source and to erupt into the patient's behavior and consciousness. Such are, for example, painful emotions like anxiety, guilt or depression; obsessions, such as a driver's idea that he is going to smash into oncoming vehicles; compulsions, as when someone must wash his hands several times an hour or feel acute anxiety. An example is a young girl of twenty who cannot stand being alone, cannot attend a service in church unless she stays close to the door (claustrophobia), cannot go out except with her sister (agoraphobia). At night she wakes up, is too hot and feels nervous; before she can go to sleep again she is forced to walk about the room for a certain time (compulsion). All her symptoms seem to her to be both irritating and incomprehensible.

To sum up, psychoneurotic symptoms can be understood as involuntary discharges that take the place of normal actions.

The Classification of Neuroses

To better understand the nature of psychoneurotic symptoms it is useful to distinguish traumatic from actual symptoms.

A traumatic neurosis is a morbid state caused by a trauma, that is, by an influx of such powerful external stimuli—by such a critical and urgent situation—that the subject finds it impossible to master these, and a discharge becomes impossible. Classical examples are furnished by neuroses following bombardment, explosions or catastrophes. A simple, familiar example is a child who is humiliated by his fellows and is not strong enough to fight back. He goes home in a state of impotent rage; he can think of nothing else and tries out repartees and attacks until things fall into place once again. The immediate effects of a trauma are sensations of painful tension, inadequate attempts to master things that cannot be mastered through normal adjustments. To this disorder in behavior are added emotional discharges, broken sleep on account of excessive tension, symptoms of repetition of the trauma either in sleep or awake, repetitions aimed at mastering the conflict, and finally, in cases of failure, psychoneurotic symptoms, varying in kind with constitutional factors and previous experiences.

The notion of an actual neurosis was suggested early on by Freud, during the period when he outlined the concept of a neurosis of defense (1894). The conflict is determined, not by an assault of external stimulation, but by actual internal stimulation due to the tension of needs not adequately discharged. The classical example is sexual intercourse that does not end in a satisfactory orgasm (*coitus interruptus*). During analysis the liberation of impulses that do not have an outlet can produce "actual" symptoms. Negative symptoms (fatigue and fatigability, loss of interest, boredom, inferiority feelings) and positive symptoms (a general state of tension, disorder in muscle tone, emotional discharges in the form of anxiety and anger, insomnia, disorders in somatic functions) may both be found.

Depending on the individual's constitution and history, the clinical picture takes the form of anxiety neurosis or neurasthenia (Freud).

Psychoneurosis, properly speaking, is a more developed elaboration of conflict. Some of the more usual forms are conversion hysteria, anxiety hysteria with phobias, and obsessive neurosis. If ego defense impedes the discharge of an instinctual impulse experienced as dangerous or reprehensible, the impulse is not abolished but diverted. It finds a "substitute discharge" that is not so questionable in images and daydreams (for example, sexual, ambitious or aggressive daydreams) and sometimes breaks out into reality through some mistake or slip. The defensive blocking of the psychoneurosis prevents a sufficient discharge, and this condition determines a continuous production of actual symptoms and a state where minimal external or internal excitations are enough to put the subject in a traumatic state.

For example, a young obsessed patient avoided going out. If he happened to meet a girl who seemed to have too short a skirt on, he became upset for several hours. This defense had originally been directed against incestuous desires liable to be punished. Later, all sexual stirring up, even if not incestuous, assumed traumatic significance.

Thus the common factor in all three types of symptom is the disproportion between excitation and discharge, determined by the excess of external stimulation in the traumatic neurosis, the interruption of the discharge process in the actual neurosis, and the defensive block against discharge in the psychoneurosis. Clinically this similarity comes out in an overlap among the three types of neurosis. Psychoneuroses deserve their name, because they represent a psychological elaboration of neurotic conflict. They are attempts at adjustment that, thanks to the symptoms, reconcile satisfaction and security even though discharge is inadequate and the symptom (through the discomfort it produces) becomes a secondary source of difficulty.

The Cause of Psychoneuroses

A psychoneurosis is the product of the interaction between the personality and the environment.

The personality plays a major role. There is no psychoneurosis without a neurotic predisposition, and more precisely, without an infantile neurosis.

Contrary to the widely held view, psychoanalysis takes the constitutional factor into account. But it does not hasten to resort to this, considering it to be the limit of psychoanalytic investigations. Also, individuals are unequally sensitive to the effects of frustration or excessive excitation, since nervous systems are unequally excitable or delicate, and genital needs or aggressive responses vary greatly in strength. On the other hand, all these somatic factors are influenced by the vicissitudes of the individual's history.

The real discovery of psychoanalysis is the determining role of infantile neurosis, the fixation points that dominate, and the characteristic mechanisms of the developmental period in which fixation occurs, in short, of the nature and role of the infantile environment. Fixation can arise either from severe frustration and a corresponding development of phantasy, or from an excessive satisfaction that subsequently decreases frustration tolerance.

Karl Abraham has arranged the fixation points characteristic of the different mental illnesses in a schema that places them parallel to the corresponding stages in the development of impulses and object relations (1924). To Freud, the Oedipus complex is the central point in neurosis. But the Oedipus complex is also part of normal development, although it is surpassed and then can no longer manifest itself except in such favorable conditions as dreams. With neurotics, the Oedipus complex is not resolved because of the particular intensity of the impulses, the affects and the defenses that go to its making. In certain hysterias Oedipal fixation is the essence of the pathogenesis. But the abnormal evolution of the Oedipus complex can itself be the result of preceding difficulties. Classically these are considered the pre-Oedipal difficulties. According to Melanie Klein and her school, the Oedipal conflict arises in the earliest stages of development.

The role of the environment is that of a factor intervening through frustration. Sometimes it is a case of a clearcut, brutal event of unusual significance; for example, the death of a loved one. In other cases the neurosis develops insidiously owing to a situation of prolonged frustration; for example, an unhappy marriage, or some minor event that happens to have a specific meaning.

The Formation of Psychoneurotic Symptoms

If the subject is without predispositions, he can endure such frustration and make a well-adapted response, for example, by finding a new object of love. But instead, as a result of neurotic tendencies, he may respond by a partial withdrawal of interest in the external world and an increase in phantasy activity. Impulses free themselves from reality relations and ego control. The subject falls back on a more secure position resulting from more primitive interests, and this regression does not stop until the fixation point is reached, that is, until the stage where libidinal and aggressive impulses toward familial objects were overtaxed. But this regression is not total. To a large extent the ego continues to function normally and to bring its defense mechanisms into play against expressions deriving from repressed impulses. The failure of some defenses brings others into action.

As in the dream, repressed wishes cannot manifest themselves directly, but only in substitute and disguised ways. The symptom is also a rejection of these unconscious wishes, which becomes clear when the symptom implies physical or moral discomfort or seriously compromises ego functioning (self-punishment). It is a compromise between repressed factors and the ego defense. All these factors are unconscious, but preconscious and conscious activity is made use of as part of the compromise, exactly as in the dream. One of the best examples of this secondary elaboration is furnished by the obsessed person, who uses his logical powers to justify the extension of his thoughts and obsessive rituals. Because of the symptom formation (for lack of a successful repression), the neurotic gets a certain abatement in unconscious tension; this is the primary gain from a neurosis. Secondary gain comes from the patient's being able to influence his environment, through tyrannizing over it in revenge.

These two gains encourage the neurotic to compromise with the symptom. He often develops a sort of attachment to it, whatever the inconvenience, and resists all efforts to suppress it, feeling a sense of loss if the symptom begins to disappear.

Psychoses

The term *psychosis* is applied to major behavior disorders—manifested in perceptual distortions of reality and loss of self-control—so serious that they justify confinement; in a word, to "madness." "Functional" psychoses are those in which the importance of personal and social factors is greater than explanations arising from pathological anatomy, physiology or biochemistry. Freud was interested in the psychoses from early in his career (1896), seeing in them the defense of the organism against disappointment inflicted by reality. The general concept of psychosis is superimposed on that of neurosis, but with important differences. Fixation and regression are deeper; frustration and trauma are relatively more severe in relation to ego tolerance; the ego turns away from reality and allows itself to be subjugated by the id; and affective interest, instead of recoiling on imaginary objects, recoils on the ego. Freud summed up his views in the idea that in psychoses the conflict lies between the ego and reality, while in neuroses it lies between the ego and the id (1924). Yet this distinction is only relative: conflict between the ego and reality is also present in the neuroses, while in the psychoses reality still represents objects toward which instinctual impulses tend, objects that are the sources of temptation.

Psychoanalysis has made an important contribution to the psychology of "organic processes"—psychic disorders mainly determined by somatic causes and cerebral impairment. When Freud was attempting to differentiate neurosis and psychosis, he took as an example of psychosis Meynert's "amentia" (acute mental confusion), a disease with undoubted somatic elements. The psychoanalyst's orientation toward an explanation of concrete behavior puts him in a good position to advance psychological research on psychotic reactions caused by organic processes. Schilder especially has made important contributions to the psychology of general paralysis (1928). Electroshock therapy and neurosurgery have opened up new fields for psychoanalytic research.

The manic-depressive psychosis, isolated by classic psychiatry, manifests itself by phases of melancholy depression or manic elation, separated by free periods. Whatever such a "morbid entity" (distinct from schizophrenia) may be—and many clinicians accept it only with reservations—most psychoanalysts remain faithful to an "organic" aetiology. But a clear-cut distinction between organic and psychological explanations is more logical than realistic. For where emotional disorders are mainly in question we must ask ourselves what melancholia or mania would be without bodily participation. On the other hand, the discoveries of Freud, Abraham and others allow us to enter into the psychology of depressed and elated states and to understand the genesis of the patient's personality.

Predisposition may be found in patients' feelings regarding their own existence and worth; such patients are extremely dependent on external support or personal self-satisfaction. In other words, there is an exaggerated need for affection and esteem. Their intolerance to loss of love and humiliating frustrations easily makes them aggressive, but their aggression is largely blocked because of their fear of losing another's love and their sense of guilt, so that it tends to rebound against themselves. This predisposition is related to fixation at the oral-sadistic stage, when an ambivalent object relation develops through incorporation. It makes such people especially sensitive to loss of self-esteem or love, and to everything that stimulates their guilt feelings, either through apparent traumata or through very slight and disguised events, the existence and importance of which only psychoanalytic investigation can reveal. For example, a patient entered a depressed phase one day during the Christmas season because she had not been invited to a family dinner. Many authors (Freud, Abraham, Lagache) have stressed the part mourning plays, when its nature is brutal, in determining depressed or elated reactions. The nature of the predisposition and the precipitating factors makes it understandable why melancholia is especially expressed in sentiments of guilt and annihilation, in self-punitive reactions, delirious ideas of self-accusation, and suicide. The structure of the depressed state is complicated by the patient's identification with the lost love object. Self-aggression is directed against the ego, "modified by the shadow of the object." A depressed woman found in herself all the faults with which she charged her son, who had been killed instantly in an automobile accident (Lagache, 1938). Thus melancholia represents, from the functional point of view, a sort of labor through which the depressed person tries painfully to resolve conflicts of old standing that have been reactivated by recent events. Mania has the same basic problems, but the patient tries to free himself by "a flight toward reality." One might call it an "all-the-same" technique. One patient, during a manic attack following her father's suicide, cried out: "I've had enough of a heredity like that!" (1937).

In the schizophrenias, we find clinical pictures that cannot be completely reduced to psychological comprehension (Jaspers). The ideas of Bleuler are opposed to Kraepelinian theory on dementia praecox, which Kraepelin conceived of as a mental illness that starts in youth and results in dementia. For Bleuler, schizophrenia can begin at any age, and can be cured; despite the vagueness of neuropathological data, the hypothesis of a cerebral defect cannot be eliminated, but personality and circumstances also play an important part. Bleuler himself emphasized his debt to psychoanalysis, and especially to Jung (1911). The psychoanalytic contribution forms an essential part of the general theory of the group of schizophrenias. According to Abraham, the principal fixation takes place at an even earlier date than in manic-depressive psychosis—in fact, at the oral sucking stage, when the ego has not yet been differentiated from reality. It is thought that predisposition is due to various combinations among somatic tendencies, early traumata, and manifold obstacles, especially in the orientation toward objects. Other fixations, especially Oedipal conflicts, play a secondary role. As in the neuroses, the precipitating factor is either an increase in impulse tension (puberty), a traumatic stimulation of repressed infantile sexuality (homosexuality, anality), or any other circumstance that justifies or increases the reasons for an infantile defense. As in the neuroses, the subject tends to integrate tension through regression, with the difference that here regression takes the form of a break with reality. Reality is rejected insofar as it is a source both of frustration and temptation, that is, insofar as it conceals objects toward which impulses are directed. The ego tends to be submerged by the id. From this arises "de-differentiation" and "primitivation" of behavior, which are expressed in phantasies of world destruction, depersonalization, ideas of grandeur, archaic modes of thought and speech, hebephrenic symptoms and certain catatonic ones. Another part of the clinical picture corresponds to an attempt at a cure, an impulse effort to defeat frustrating reality and attain satisfaction (hallucinations, delirium, verbal or social peculiarities, various catatonic symptoms).

Psychoanalysts generally consider "paranoid psychoses" as circumscribed schizophrenias. Psychoses are so called when they appear as "personality developments" (Jaspers) at grips with life situations and expressed principally in the "chronic systematic delusions" of the older writers, or in delusional ideas of persecution, grandeur, guilt and the like that develop without any gross impairment of intelligence. These are the "sane" madnesses. Psychoanalytic discoveries have largely contributed to the conception of these as psychological developments; this in no way precludes probable but little-known somatic determinants.

We shall take the delusion of persecution as an example. The basic work here is Freud's psychoanalytic commentary (1911) on the autobiography of a magistrate, Dr. jur. Daniel Paul Schreber. Freud demonstrates that the idea of persecution represents a defense against a father complex and in particular against the passive homosexual component in infantile sexuality. It is the result of a double mechanism of negation (I do not love him, I hate him) and projection (I hate him because he is persecuting me). Defense against unconscious homosexuality also enters into erotomania and jealousy. Additional proof is furnished by the fact that during the treatment of homosexuality we can see the episodic intervention of unmotivated jealousy (Lagache, 1949). Observation of numerous cases leads to the general proposition that the persecutor is a homosexual object. Homosexuality is an intermediary position between narcissism and heterosexuality, indicative either of regression or re-evolution. Dutch psychoanalysts have shown the existence of fixation at the early anal stage, where the incorporation of the object and its subsequent destruction are accomplished through the anus. Other forms of incorporation also intervene. As a result, the persecutor not only represents a homosexual object but also a personal trait or a bodily part superimposed and projected upon the person of the persecutor, especially the feces and the buttocks. The persecution is comparable to intestinal sensations.

Finally, this reprojection of personal traits or bodily parts onto an external person bears on the superego. Ideas of persecution, influence, guilt, voices, the echo of thought, commentary on actions—all correspond to a projection into the social sphere of attitudes of self-observation and self-criticism. We can see the part played by the establishment of the superego in the development of these attitudes. The superego is in general the result of an identification with an object of the same sex. Thus we return by another route to the idea that the persecutor is a homosexual object.

Psychoanalysis of the psychoses has enjoyed a new

vogue for several years, but it is difficult to sort out the dominant directions in a wealth of clinical and therapeutic work.

Perversions

These fall into two categories: (1) disorders in sexual behavior, mainly characterized by anomalies in the sexual object or goal (for example, homosexuality, fetishism, sadism and masochism); (2) "irresistible" habits, of which drug addiction and dipsomania are the most frequent examples.

The point of departure for psychoanalytic theory was the discovery of infantile sexuality and of the identity of the pervert's sexual goals with those of children (Freud, 1905); the linking of perversion and the neurotic symptom followed as a consequence of this. The pervert is a subject who has regressed to an infantile form of behavior after frustration; the psychoneurotic symptom is also a response to frustration, but it is different from regression, or is indeed a defense against regression; and so neurosis is "a negative form of perversion."

But such a concept is inadequate. Perverse sexuality is not polymorphous and unorganized, like that of the child; nor is it limited to preliminary pleasure. The only difference is that the dominant behavior that allows genital orgasm is not the genital behavior of the adult, but a perverse behavior. In typical perversions it is Oedipal conflict that prevents the primacy of normal genital behavior, with an intensity of castration anxiety and guilt feelings. If perverse behavior makes orgasm possible, it is because in the moment of satisfaction it also constitutes a defense against castration and certain repressed elements of infantile sexuality. The fixative action of infantile sexual experiences is bound up with the fact that they unite satisfaction and security.

Let us examine a case of masculine homosexuality in order to understand this mechanism better. The patient, a man of about thirty, had as partners young people toward whom he behaved in a strictly active way (sucking the penis, swallowing sperm, phantasies about cutting off the penis). *Horror feminae* and impotence was connected with intense castration anxiety, which was also connected with a passive father fixation that had been deeply repressed. Thus the "pseudo-active" homosexual behavior not only represented satisfaction but was also a defense against passive homosexuality and a negation of castration fears, especially thanks to the identification with the masculine partner magically realized by oral incorporation.

Thus we find, in sexual perversions, that compromise between satisfaction and defense which is characteristic of neurotic conflict. All the same, in the "impulsive neuroses" (for example, toxicomania or dipsomania) non-sexual satisfaction or the disguised satisfaction of aggressive or sexual tendencies combines with defense against an unconscious danger, a menace to the narcissistic need for affection, approval and security. Extreme dependence is connected with oral fixation—a synthesis of satisfaction and security—and it is this that makes such patients akin to depressed ones. Emotionally, toxicomania and the dipsomanic crisis are often defenses against depression.

For example, one alcoholic patient sacrificed everything—wife, children, job, fortune, reputation—to his need for drink. An anxiety neurotic tortured by timidity, his dipsomania stopped when pulmonary tuberculosis made a cure in a sanatorium necessary and placed him once again in the passive and receptive situation characteristic of early infancy.

Character Neuroses

These are neuroses in which psychoneurotic symptoms are replaced by pathological personality behavior traits, by *character disorders*. These disorders are mainly marked by rigidity of response both to external and internal stimulation, with a consequent decrease in the plasticity and richness of the personality.

Like the psychoneurotic symptom, the pathological behavior trait rests essentially on a defense against *an unconscious wish* and has its origin in an infantile neurosis. If the dangerous impulse can neither be satisfied, sublimated or integrated in a neurotic symptom, the only solution is to act against it, and this reaction can take either the form of inhibition or of reaction formation. Behavior is complicated by more or less disfigured expressions of the repressed impulse or by a secondary defense against the primary one. For example, affective frigidity and intellectualization constitute a defense against a fear of emotionality. A man can defend himself against castration anxiety by developing passive, feminine tendencies, and then react against this defense by adopting a "superman" form of behavior. Conduct in which pity is extremely outstanding is probably connected with original sadistic tendencies. One of the most typical examples is that of ascetic personalities who spend their lives battling their impulses. The genesis and dynamics of these pathological behavior traits make it possible to consider them neurotic. The main difference between them and psychoneurotic symptoms is their permanence and the fact that they are not usually considered to be strange; this is why they are difficult to analyze. Indeed it is not possible to do so unless the latent conflict is intensified and the analysand can manage to place it at a distance. The importance of character neuroses has become increasingly apparent during the last twenty years. The development of psychoanalysis has put ego analysis and analysis of the mechanisms of defense first. On the other hand, the neuroses themselves have developed. Neuroses with clear-cut symptoms in relation to the personality, such as hysterical symptoms, belong to an epoch when the educative attitude in relation to impulses was itself clearly defined. Since moral education has become more indecisive, the neurotic personality has become more inconsistent, and symptoms have become more fluid and more mixed up with the total personality.

In a general way, different neuroses correspond to societies' different value systems and educational methods: "The instability of contemporary society is characterized by conflicts between the ideal of individual liberty, determined by the aspirations of capitalism, and the regressive need for passive dependence, determined by the individual's helplessness over what concerns the distribution of wealth or security, no less than by educational measures that result from the social necessity of authority" (Fenichel, 1945). Conflict between the need for dependence and the need for independence is at the heart of many character disorders.

Criminal Behavior

Psychoanalysis has played a decisive part in stimulating criminology, by orienting it toward the study of the personality and behavior of the criminal (Healy, De Greeff). It is mainly since the twenties that research has become intense in this sphere, both on adults (Reik, Alexander and Staub, Alexander and Healy) and on children and adolescents (Aichhorn, Zulliger, Schmiedeberg, Friedlander, Bowlby).

Difficulties arise from the connection with social and especially psychological conditions, that is, from the criminal's attitude to his action, which is not experienced as either painful or culpable. Undoubtedly—in 20 per cent of all cases—the criminal is sick.

Among pathological crimes the neurotic crime is an action maladapted to reality and motivated by the wish to reduce internal tension. The explanation of crime as due to a pre-existing guilt feeling (suggested by Freud in 1915) can be verified in some cases, but often neurotic mechanisms intervene. Most often criminals are, to begin with, comparable to the rest of the population. They obey motivations that others are usually prevented from obeying through fear or through respect for others.

Thus the problem is one of transition into action. This clears up when we consider that every action implies a hierarchy of values. The criminal acts on an individual code of values, or the code of a group, usually a group that is under restraint because of its connection with a more widespread society. Membership in a group depends mainly on identification, and in normal development the personality becomes socialized through identification. Predisposition to criminal behavior depends on anomalies in socialization, identification and superego formation. At this point, whatever the part played by heredity, differentiation of constitutional predispositions cannot come about except through a learning process. Different happenings may be met with. In certain cases identification is accomplished through a person or a group whose code of values is not that of the community. For example, a child may be brought up by parents who are thieves. Or identification may be made with the worst side of some member of the environment or with a pathological personality. The most widespread and best-known case seems to be that in which educational conditions during early childhood (frequent changes, lack of love, inconsistent education) do not allow the development of stable affective relations with the environment, and the mother in particular. From this spring inadequacies or anomalies of identification and of the formation of the superego, revolt against authority, persistence of the infantile ideal of omnipotence, and sado-masochistic relations with others.

A careful study of the biographies of young delinquents is often enough to show the causes of criminal behavior. In a good investigation Bowlby compared a group of forty-four young recidivist thieves with an equivalent group of forty-four maladjusted children. A statistical study of the clinical and biographical data showed, in the case of the thieves, that an "indifferent" type frequently occurred, and that among this type severe disturbance of the mother-child relation (for example, on account of prolonged stays in hospital) was often to be found. Instead of learning to substitute the need to be loved and approved of by the mother for the immediate satisfaction of all its needs, these children had become inextricably involved in a web of disappointments, rages, guilt feelings and indifference, which constitute a defense against both disappointment and aggression.

Theft, which is often theft of food or of money to buy food, represents an equivalent for maternal love. Other works on this subject (especially those of Spitz) show that unfavorable educational conditions in very early infancy have consequences not only for identification but also for the whole development of the organism. In effect, a study of the criminal personality often shows ego inadequacies, such as defects in judgment and incapacity to benefit from experience or to anticipate the future.

We can sum up the dominant ideas of psychoanalytic research on this subject by saying that the disposition to criminal behavior depends mainly on a perpetuation of infantile egocentricity, which is bound up with anomalies in identification and consequently in socialization.

10 / Somatic Disorders

Historical Comments

This chapter is devoted to "somatic disorders" not only because of the extension of psychoanalysis during recent decades with the development of psychosomatic medicine, i.e. of "that part of medicine whose object it is to take into account simultaneously both the emotional and psychological mechanisms in the morbid processes of the individual, by stressing the mutual influences of these two factors upon one another and upon the individual, considered as a whole" (Osler). Whatever the criticisms of psychosomatic medicine, or even of the very term (Fenichel), this type of study is especially suited to a grasp of the links between psychoanalysis and biology and medicine.

One current mistake is to conceive of psychoanalysis as oriented tendentiously toward a purely psychological form of explanation. This mistake has two main sources. The first is the conceptualization and formulation of facts and hypotheses, which originated in the dichotomy between the physical and the moral; for many thinkers, to propose an explanation not purely anatomico-physiological is to opt for a psychological causality.

The other reason for error is heuristic. The exploitation of psychoanalytic hypotheses and techniques has stimulated experiments—and therefore errors—in various directions, and notably in the "psychogenic" direction. But this latter is not in any privileged position and is the basis of the criticism of Freud himself for extreme "organicism"; and it would be fairer to represent the development of psychoanalysis as a dialectic between "biologizing" and "culturizing," maturation and learning.

Critics of psychoanalysis usually have in common a stereotyped, crystallized and schematic image of the doctrine. Like other biological and psychological disciplines, psychoanalysis had difficulty in freeing itself from the dualism of the moral and the physical. But more than any other discipline, and from its very beginning, psychoanalysis represented progress in the direction of considering the totality of the organism as it is involved in different situations. From this point of view, the terminological distinction between "organism" and "personality" is purely verbal: no organism exists that does not behave in relation to situations, nor does a personality exist without a body. The organism's attempts at adjustment throw into play simultaneously both interofective mechanisms (physiological regulation) and exterofective mechanisms (behavioral acts).

These two groups of reactions are articulated, complement one another and form a whole. In the case of the animal that must either attack or flee, this produces a discharge of adrenalin and a liberation of glycogen, an increase in arterial tension, an acceleration of the pulse, a decrease in the time taken for blood to coagulate, and so on; physicochemical modifications of the organism incite the animal to action in order that it may drink, eat, mate and sleep. This distinction, made by Cannon in his books on the subject, still provides useful concepts and terms for a consideration of behavior and of disease from the point of view of the totality of the organism. Progress in our knowledge has made it possible to distinguish many categories of acts.

Conversion Hysteria

Conversion hysteria corresponds approximately to the classical type of hysteria. The most obvious symptoms of this neurosis are manifest in somatic dysfunction (for example, in paralysis or hysterical blindness), but sometimes such a chronic state may set in motion irreversible anatomical modifications. As in all neuroses, conversion hysteria represents a compromise between sexual or aggressive tendencies and ego defense. The specific factor is that the conflict finds expression in bodily symptoms, which are substitute attainments or unconscious desires and phantasies. For example, vomiting may mean "I am pregnant," a convulsion, "I am having an orgasm," blindness, "I don't want to see," abasia (finding it difficult or impossible to walk), "I want to go into forbidden places, and to avoid doing this I shall not go anywhere"; and so on. The symptom helps to lessen the strain, although only partially. Above all, the symptom has a meaning and so can be interpreted, in the same way as a dream; it is like a dream that has borrowed the language of the body's plasticity.

Some authors have extended the domain of conversion very widely indeed. Alexander would like to limit it to motor and sensory functions. Fenichel thinks that such a clear-cut delimitation is impossible. But one fact is agreed on by everybody: conversion phenomena are efforts at response and have a meaning.

Vegetative Neuroses

Alexander has laid special stress on the difference between conversion symptoms and "vegetative neuroses." In the latter, physical symptoms are not substitutes for repressed emotions, as in conversion. Rather, they are normal, physiological concomitants of emotions and constitute a preparation of the organism for action—but a preparation that is purely somatic, representing an "interofective" adjustment, as Cannon puts it.

Although the adaptation and release are complete, an "exterofective" adjustment is lacking—that is, some action adapted to reality or at least an adequate expression of emotion. The chronic nature of this condition makes it morbid and pathogenic. Here somatic symptoms do not have a psychological and symbolic meaning, but are purely the physical effects, whether direct or indirect, of conflict. So a vegetative neurosis (such as arterial hypertension) is not an attempt to express an emotion or resolve a conflict, but is the physiological accompaniment, either constant or episodic, of recurrent emotional states. For example, the author has had under observation a woman whose inhibitions and whose husband's attitude would not allow her to express her criticisms or hostile reactions; among other symptoms she developed hypertension, which disappeared after several weeks of psychoanalysis. The best known example is the peptic ulcer, especially studied by Alexander and the Chicago School. *Gastric neurosis* consists in chronic disturbance of the motor action and secretion of the stomach, and is not the expression or release of an emotion but its physiological accompaniment. It attacks patients who have the need to be loved and taken care of, who are "hungry for love," a need that they cannot satisfy on account of their guilt feelings or shame, and that therefore remains unsatisfied. This need is closely connected with the desire to be nourished, the first situation in which the child experiences the satisfaction of being loved and cared for by his mother. Thus a chronic need to be loved is adapted to stimulate the motor and secretory functions of the stomach. Gastric symptoms are the physiological corollaries of the passive expectance of food, the physiological counterpart of an emotion, and not its substitute. If the need to be loved is taken care of and satisfied one way or another (for example, thanks to hospital treatment), the symptoms disappear. Many functional disorders result in this way from an interaction of physiological and psychological mechanisms, in all fields of pathology. Even catching an infection can be given favorable conditions by emotion and arterial spasm.

The wide exploitation of "psychosomatic" hypotheses has resulted in some exaggeration and suggested reservations. Fenichel has attempted to bring some order into this subject. In that vast hinterland between conversion phenomena and somatic disorders in which a purely physiopathological explanation is most relevant, it is necessary, according to this author, to distinguish: (1) the equivalents of affects, made up from the physiological processes accompanying an emotion the psychic content of which is repressed (for example, Freud's "somatic equivalents of anxiety" or certain cardiac neuroses); (2) chemical disturbances in a frustrated person (Freud's "actual neuroses," which show themselves in a decrease of ego function because of the energy used up in conflict and through positive symptoms, such as painful sensations of tension or an incomprehensible tendency toward inadequate affective discharge in anxiety or anger); (3) the physical results of unconscious affective attitudes (for example, peptic ulcers); and (4) combinations of these different mechanisms and of conversion, such combinations appearing to be the general rule in the pathogenesis of "organic neuroses."

Somatic Illnesses

To avoid misunderstanding, it is useful to mention that the concept of a purely somatic physiopathology remains a legitimate one. The coincidence of a somatic disorder with psychological factors is not sufficient to make up an "organic neurosis." On the other hand, it is convenient to stress that even if not all somatic disorder is motivated, yet it remains motivating. Whatever happens in the organism has an effect on individual conflicts, and a dream of getting fat may precede medical discovery of a tumor. The pathological functioning of the body has direct effects on emotional life, on activity, and on the nature and intensity of impulse conflict, particularly through the intermediary action of the neurohormonal chain. But illness is also a life situation, which usually sets in motion a more or less marked narcissistic regression. It has an unconscious meaning, such as castration or predestined abandonment. The sick person may try, more or less deliberately, to aggravate the illness and take refuge in it; or the illness may rearouse an infantile neurosis or provoke a neurosis (Ferenczi's *pathoneuroses*). In other cases, the appearance of a somatic illness, by fully satisfying a masochistic need for suffering, may make a neurosis superfluous (Fenichel's *pathocure*).

Practical Problems

The part played by psychological factors in bodily disease raises several social, scientific and therapeutic problems. From the social point of view, medical progress—as in prophylaxis and the treatment of infectious diseases—has simultaneously modified the distribution of age in a given population and also its pathology; functional and chronic disorders, such as hypertension, and in general, all so-called psychosomatic disorders, have become a social scourge. As a result the general practitioner is poorly equipped to deal with the disorders he most frequently encounters in his practice, and the world needs the psychiatrist.

In the United States large-scale research projects have been undertaken to combine psychological and physiological investigations, anamneses and tests, but it is hard to see how a synthesis of their findings can be made without psychoanalysis, since it alone produces a subtle analysis of data. Efforts have been made to establish correlations between pathology and biotypology. The best substantiated results have been confined to showing connections between certain functional disorders and certain emotional constellations. From the therapeutic point of view, there are pathological states with psychological origins, which have become somatic to such an extent that immediate physical treatment has become necessary. As for psychoanalysis, it takes the form here of an analysis of investigation, to establish the weight of unconscious psychological factors and a dynamic diagnosis; symptoms having no psychological meaning need not be analyzed but will vanish when the generating attitude has been analyzed, that is, the anxiety or the obstacles opposing discharge. Principally in connection with bodily disorders that have a neurotic origin, Alexander and the Chicago School have done research on short-term psychotherapy and advocated its use. But such methods are only applicable in the case of traumatic neuroses and severe external conflicts. Psychoanalytic experience shows that those "psychosomatic" disturbances current in the course of any neurosis and every psychoanalytic cure are often based on deep-lying modifications of the personality and therefore require very detailed and lengthy treatment.

11 / Psychoanalytic Treatment

General Remarks

It is a delicate matter to explain psychoanalytic treatment, for many reasons. An abstract description cannot replace the history of a case, and still less the actual experience of an analysis. The diversity of therapeutic situations and developments defies generalization. The technique is not uniform, or rather, its relative uniformity is disguised by divergence in interpretation and formulation. There are differences between what one does and what one writes, and many things cannot be learned except by word of mouth. The elucidation of psychoanalytic treatment has allowed theories to become elaborated, but these have become necessary to understand the treatment. Finally, the technique has had its historical development; the writings of Freud himself bear witness to this. However, all the essential elements have been given by Freud, and it is possible without forcing things to find them in his *Studies in Hysteria* (1895). It is only that the relative weight attached to different elements has varied; progress in technical conceptualization and the promotion of certain theoretical concepts have determined modifications in orientation and in the question of what is of central importance. In the beginning the dominant concept was that of a dynamic unconscious, and analysis was essentially the analysis of unconscious content (Anna Freud). With the development of the topographical approach, analysis became centered in an analysis of the ego and the mechanisms of defense, stress being laid on the need for overcoming resistance before unconscious content. In the last two decades theoretical interest has turned to object relations, both external and internal; technically, attention has been given to the intercommunication between the patient and the analyst.

The technique can certainly develop further. Once this has been said, there remains a corpus of information and ideas held in common. The technique has reached a degree of maturity and stability that makes it possible to describe certain of its general traits.

Initial Interviews

Psychoanalysis is a medical treatment and should not be used without a preliminary clinical examination by a competent physician. The psychiatrist knows that psychoneuroses, inhibitions and psychosexual or character disorders are more accessible to psychoanalysis than are delinquency or psychosis. An experienced psychoanalytic doctor can better evaluate the chances of a successful analysis, since these depend not only on diagnosis but also on the possibilities and limitations of the client, on life conditions, on future perspectives, and on the patient's capacity for communication.

Intensive study of individual cases belongs to the clinical method, and in this sense psychoanalysis is "ultra-clinical." However, the initial interview is different from that of the ordinary psychiatric examination. By reason of the attention that must be paid from the very beginning to the interaction between analyst and patient, the psychoanalyst carries out his examination with many precautions (for example, in his way of asking and answering questions).

If psychoanalysis is clearly indicated, it is best not to prolong the initial interviews. If indications are more doubtful, the treatment may be started on the understanding that it is for a trial period. If the diagnosis is even more tentative and the prognosis less certain—for example, if there is reason to suspect psychosis (say, schizophrenia), or that the symptoms may be due to an organic process (say, epilepsy) —it is best to have recourse to all clinical and laboratory resources, even if it may become necessary later to send the client to another psychoanalyst. In other words, psychoanalysis is not undertaken without being in possession, if not of all the facts, at least of sufficient facts.

Certain authors have advocated a deeper investigation of the illness and of the personality and biography of the client, in order to acquire as soon as possible an overview of the whole case and to plan the treatment, so as to shorten it by using the theory of the neuroses (Alexander). This "strategy" is attractive but hazardous. The nodal point of the neurosis is not the Oedipus complex in general but some particular form of it, or of a "basic neurosis" that is deeper-lying and of earlier origin. The patient can learn to master unconscious conflicts only gradually, by being confronted with them in new, different situations. In the present state of our knowledge the patient chimney-sweeping operations of psychoanalytic treatment appear to be always necessary.

Despite the precautions that must be taken, the analyst owes the patient, on a rational basis, some minimum explanation of his case and of the goals and methods of the treatment. One question that must nearly always be met is that of duration of treatment. Here the analyst can only be reserved. A psychological structure that has been maintained for years, or dozens of years, is not likely to disappear very rapidly. Two years can be named as something approximate, nothing more. It is all the better if an improvement takes place before there is any question of cure or of ending the treatment. The patient is warned of the danger of making any fundamental changes in his life before the treatment is over or sufficiently advanced. For one, in the beginning he is not in a condition to do so. Secondly, during the course of the treatment the analysis may change him in a transitory fashion. Finally, recourse to an impulsive action in real life, the hope of cutting the Gordian knot, is resistance to the resolution of unconscious conflict. Sharp conflict, an urgent need to make a decision, are not matters for analysis, and it is necessary to postpone either the treatment or the decision. So, finally, after the initial interviews, analyst and patient conclude all the arrangements about time and number of weekly sessions, fees and all foreseeable interruptions of treatment (such as journeys and holidays).

External Conditions of Treatment

Originally, daily analytic sessions were usual. Today it is thought best not to have fewer than four or five weekly sessions for as long as possible; and three is the minimum allowed by many analysts. A more sustained rhythm facilitates the resolution of difficulties and the development of the treatment; too, it is plain that the more the analyst sees his patient, the more he can follow him from close at hand. Each session lasts forty-five or fifty minutes. Neither the frequency nor the length of the sessions can be decreased very much without altering the nature of analytic treatment. The patient stretches out on a couch and the analyst sits down behind him—a situation that allows the patient to avoid all postural effort and to speak without having to face the analyst and without knowing anything about his reactions (also, the analyst thus need not control his attitude and facial expression, which frees him to listen, observe and interpret). These conditions are essential for the typical treatment, although certain therapeutic situations make necessary such changes as a face-to-face position.

The Fundamental Rule

This is the rule of free association, in which the patient is instructed. He is told to say "everything that passes through his mind," to express verbally what he thinks and feels without choosing anything or excluding anything of his own free will, even if what emerges seems unpleasant, absurd, futile or pointless. In fact, no one can talk without choosing and excluding, and literally there is no free association, since the association of ideas is determined, and for this very reason is revealing. The fundamental rule seeks only to eliminate voluntary selection—the conscious choice and ordering of thought—so as to afford favorable conditions for involuntary expression. In this way ego defenses and unconscious themes appear that interfere with the verbal expression of all the patient's potentialities. Silences, facial expressions, gestures and attitudes make up another language that supplements the spoken word or substitutes for it. The interpretation and working through of the resistance allows the patient gradually to eliminate associative interference. Learning the fundamental rule is learning freedom in self-expression and communication with another.

The Analyst's Role

The analyst's role is to observe, listen and understand, to know how to keep silent and when is the right moment for giving a suitable interpretation. Freud has summed this up in well-known formulae. He warns against a strained attention and recommends a "floating attention," which allows a more receptive understanding and responds to the free association demanded by the patient. Freud advises the analyst to be like a mirror, reflecting nothing but what it is shown. The analyst reveals nothing of himself, of his life or his opinions. Autoanalysis should allow him to control interference from his personal and emotional reactions (countertransference). To counsel or direct the patient would be incompatible with the spontaneity demanded of him and could only bring out the patient's dependence or arouse his opposition. But if the analyst's role is not an authoritarian one, neither is it laissez-faire. The treatment must be brought as soon as possible into a state of "abstinence," which means that the energy necessary to the treatment must not escape into substitute satisfactions, either within the treatment or outside it. The analyst may thus be led to advise against, or forbid, activities pathological or normal that function as neurotic defenses, although usually not until after allowing these expression in analysis. Thus the arrangement of the psychoanalytic environment and the analyst's technical role work together to diminish the usual social ties and ego control, and the analytic state may be compared with the hypnotic one. In recent years stress has been laid on the "de-real," infantile aspects of the psychoanalytic situation, and this process of putting reality in parentheses is a condition for the development of the treatment. We must not forget that the patient also finds in this freedom, security and unusual understanding, and that the analyst, despite his invisibility and silence, is strangely present to him.

Transference and the Transference Neurosis

All psychotherapy depends on the relation between therapist and patient. It substitutes a therapeutic or transference neurosis for the clinical neurosis. The proper function of psychoanalysis is to control, interpret and treat the transference neurosis.

Analytic transference is usually defined as the repetition *vis-à-vis* the analyst of the unconscious emotional attitudes—friendly, hostile or ambivalent—that the patient established in his childhood during his contact with his parents and others in his environment. This definition lights up an essential aspect of transference: the patient should make the repetition through action instead of acknowledging it in thought or word. But repetition in the therapeutic relationship does not show the full extent of transference.

Transference is really the actualization in the psychoanalytic situation of an unconscious problem the roots of which are in childhood.

To return to the clinical neurosis: As a result of frustration endured in reality, the patient has regressed to a fixation point that corresponds to the most significant problems of childhood. His neurotic symptoms are a compromise between the forces of ego defense and aspirations toward the discharge of repressed tendencies. Far from being satisfying, this compromise is painful, and, consciously, the patient wishes to get well.

So there the patient is, in the psychoanalytic situation, with the chance to express all his aspirations freely. Ego defenses oppose his capacity to become conscious of his unconscious conflict, to formulate it and communicate it. He sees it and acts it out (according to the means of expression the situation allows him) in analytic terms, that is, in the form of symbolic equivalents. The daughter of a dominating and violent father accuses the analyst of not allowing her any freedom and of putting pressure on her. The son of a taciturn man who did not spend time with his children seeks to capture the analyst's interest and to get his active intervention. Thus the transference neurosis, if it accurately translates a recalled defeat, pushes unconscious conflict toward the actual reality of the analytic situation. The role of interpretation is to bring this active repetition to the level of thought, acknowledgment and communication.

The production of the transference proceeds from the interaction of the patient's personality and the analytic technique. Disposition toward transference resides principally in the fact that the patient's ego reactivates once more the infantile conflict that was the focal point of the neurosis. But the analytic environment is ambiguous, both encouraging and deceiving. Repressed aspirations are acknowledged but not satisfied. Frustrations arising from the rule of abstinence push the patient to more and more primitive problems and more and more regressive forms of the transference neurosis.

Transference neurosis has both positive and negative results. As the analyst approaches areas where repressed aspirations are concealed, all the defensive forces that motivated repression rebel against his efforts and become manifest in a defensive transference. Interpretation sheds light on such resistance and on the varied forms through which it is obstinately repeated (elaboration). Gradually unconscious conflict—that is, the infantile neurosis—becomes expressed in more and more identifiable form. The positive effects of transference stand out, as the return, the beginning again of that which was repressed and often hardly even sketched in outline. Then it becomes possible to dissociate those frozen potentialities from the past and to reinvest them in new objects that offer the patient a present and a future.

This is why the analysis of transference does not constitute a particular stage in the treatment, as is sometimes said. It has to begin, insofar as the situation prepares for it, from the very onset of the treatment, and must follow on right up to its termination. It is thanks to the transference that the analyst can diminish and reduce the generating conflicts of the neurosis. As Freud said in 1912:

It is the battlefield on which victory is won, an expression of a lasting improvement in the neurosis. It is undeniable that a conquest of transference manifestations brings the analyst the greatest of difficulties. But it must not be forgotten that it is these and only these manifestations that render the inestimable help of actualizing and making evident loving emotions that have been buried and forgotten; since, in the last resort, nothing can be put to death *in absentia* and *in effigie*.

This passage from Freud is among those that insist most clearly on the importance of transference in psychoanalysis. Present-day analysts are even more categorical here, since they formulate an even wider concept of transference, including in it aggressive emotions and the habitual forms of ego defense.

Therapeutic Achievements

The wide scope and complexity of observation make it difficult to speak of therapeutic achievements in general terms. Psychoanalytic treatment is nothing less than the application of a standard technique to well-defined clinical forms. Numerous factors alter the therapeutic situation: the form the illness takes, differences in technique, the personalities of analyst and patient and their interaction, favorable or unfavorable external circumstances, the advantages and disadvantages of a cure, and so on.

This brings up the question of the psychoanalytic concept of mental health and the criteria for ending the analysis. It is generally admitted that about a fifth of all analyses can be considered as technically finished. The disappearance of symptoms is not a decisive factor, since the patient can have a "flight into health" to escape analysis or to please the analyst; such flights are due to unconscious motives that interfere with genuine cures. The disappearance of symptoms is only significant if it coincides with structural modifications of the personality—in analytic terms, if the conscious takes the place of the unconscious, or better, if there is fulfilled Freud's dictum that "Where id was, ego shall be," i.e. that the ego shall no longer be in the power of the id and the superego or of repetition compulsion, and that the reality principle shall replace the pleasure principle. Such a state of affairs is reflected in certain psychological signs, of which we shall list here the most important:

1. Freedom from anxiety over frustration; the capacity to produce and tolerate strong tension and reduce it in a satisfactory way.

2. The suppression of inhibitions and a capacity to realize one's potentialities; normal sexuality and the freeing of constructive aggression and of affective and imaginative functions.

3. The adjustment of aspirations to a level suited to the person's abilities and to reality.

4. An ability to behave according to a long-term view of the results of one's actions and to work toward the realization of a life plan.

5. Improvement of relations with others.

6. Forsaking exaggeratedly conformist or destructive attitudes and finding a reconciliation between conservative and creative forces.

It is certainly rare when such a program is fully realized. Both analyst and patient must watch for illusions of perfectionism and of the omnipotence of analysis. Therefore it is difficult to appreciate at what moment the treatment has produced the results reasonably to be expected, so as to avoid either over-prolonging the analysis or terminating it too soon.

Despite the outstanding difficulties, there is a remarkable convergence in independent statistics, so that R. P. Knight (1941) was able to combine these. In psychoneuroses, inhibitions, psychosexual disturbances, character disorders and somatic disorders originating in conflict, the percentage of cure or great improvement is comparable to that obtained by therapy in the other branches of medicine. Aggravation of the illness is exceptional. With suicidal patients, the risk of death is almost negligible during the course of treatment, and only necessitates special precautions during interruptions in treatment.

Is the cure brought about by a complete analysis a final one? In principle, yes, and facts largely confirm this conjecture. However, Freud qualified this opinion (1937), warning that it always remains possible that certain unconscious conflicts have not been sufficiently reactivated, either because of the conditions of the patient's life or because of the particular conditions of the therapeutic situation. A relapse is therefore possible, less on account of serious trials than because of specific circumstances calculated to reawaken the infantile neurosis.

Healing Mechanisms

The theory of therapeutic results is difficult. This is because the treatment is long and complex, with many intervening factors, some of which are external to the treatment; because the same mechanisms can be now pathogenic, now normative; and because it is not easy to discern in the midst of these numerous factors precisely which ones are analytic.

Two opposed prejudices should be avoided. The first is to conceive of analysis as a psychological and completely intellectual treatment; analysis is an experience, a match played between the patient and analyst, and there is no genuine analysis without the development and resolution of defensive conflicts caused by alterations in the patient's mode of being and behaving. The other prejudice consists in thinking of analysis as an emotional discharge, while abreaction produces only transitory and precarious results. The genuine issue is the patient's alternation between the unthinking existence of the ego, which lives, feels and acts, and the thinking attitude of the ego, which ponders, understands and judges. The role of interpretation is to allow a development of problems and an integration of their solution, by returning to the same conflicts and the same defenses for as long as necessary. The presence of the psychoanalyst, his substitution for the patient's strict superego, the identification of the patient with the analyst as an autonomous subject: all play an important part. The gradual learning of freedom of expression and the establishing of adequate intercommunication may be considered the essential methods of the treatment and also the criteria of its evolution.

12 / Variations in Psychoanalytic Treatment

Plasticity or Rigidity

Among other criticisms of psychoanalysis, there is often the accusation of rigidity. Sometimes this is made by patients who try thus to force the analyst to set aside the rigor and reserve imposed by his technique. In fact, Freud himself, while formulating certain "rules," always considered that their application must fit in with the diversity of various therapeutic situations, for example, by rationing what one refuses (rule of abstinence) and what one accords the patient (rule of the minimum). The psychoanalyst remains such just so long as he abstains from intervening in any way, except to interpret resistance and transference, or to set up some part of unconscious material in a revealing light. And the choice, the time, the formulation of such interpretations already offers the practitioner a large measure of technical plasticity. However, with the aim of answering certain needs, variations in analytic treatment have been worked out. These are mainly used in three special cases:

psychic disorders of children, psychoses (especially schizo-phrenia) and delinquency.

The Psychoanalysis of Children

The child does not lend himself well to the require-ments of the typical treatment, that is, to free verbalization in a lying-down position, without seeing the analyst. So, without giving up verbal expression, the analyst of children is led to bring out other ways of self-expression, such as drawing, modeling or play. The nature of the treatment is not radically changed by an alteration in the means of ex-pression. But does it perhaps, for more profound reasons, derive from other principles than those behind adult analy-sis? Since 1920 controversy has centered on this theme, and from it the psychoanalysis of children has developed. From that time until her death, Melanie Klein defended the con-tention that the criteria of the Freudian psychoanalytic method, and principally the use of transference and of re-sistance, are maintained in all their integrity through play technique.

For Anna Freud (1926) the therapeutic problem is, however, different. The primitive objects of the child's con-flict are still present in his environment and have not been internalized by the definitive formation of the superego. As a result the child cannot develop a transference neurosis in the same way as the adult. The child does not come of his own accord, with the motive of getting better, but is brought by his parents. The analyst should remain in con-tact with the child's environment, or he will have only the material of dreams and daydreams at his disposal.

For all these reasons, the analyst must be "anything rather than a shadow." Besides his role as analyst he must assume the role of instructor. Technically the treatment falls into two phases. The first has the aim of destroying the negative transference and encouraging a positive one; the second alone is properly analytic. The principles of a preparatory phase and an educative influence, the destruction of the negative transference and the creation of a positive one, seem to Melanie Klein obstructions against establishing a genuine psychoanalytic situation. To her, the real analytic work is to analyze the negative transference, which then reinforces the positive transference—a reinforcement itself followed by a reinforcement of the negative transference. This different concept of child analysis is linked to a different concept of child development. According to Melanie Klein, the child is in rapport with objects from birth, and internalizes them precociously. From the end of the first year the Oedipus complex develops and the superego begins to be established. The actual love objects of a young patient are already images of original objects, whence the possibility of a transference neurosis, in which the role of the analyst is in principle the same as in an adult analysis. Anna Freud comes close to accepting such technical conceptions, while maintaining that if transference exists in child analysis, it is not properly speaking a transference neurosis. Frequently, through the spread of psychological and pedagogic knowledge, the analyst can now do without playing the instructor's role; and an analysis of initial resistance makes it possible to shorten the first part of the treatment and sometimes even to omit it (1946). Such a technical agreement does not imply the abrogation of fundamental differences as regards conceptions of early development.

Psychoanalysis of the Psychoses

The psychoses, and schizophrenia in particular, present other difficulties. Classically, Freud considered the psychoses as narcissistic types of neurosis, producing a therapeutic situation in which transference does not occur, or occurs only in such a negative or ambivalent form that psychoanalytic treatment becomes impossible. In fact, progress in our knowledge has shown that the narcissistic regression is not complete, and that neither the ego nor relations with reality are completely abolished. The psychoanalyst has to find support in these relics. The transference of infantile conflict is possible but is labile; the patient reacts to frustration by withdrawing from reality and so from the transference. Ways of meeting these difficulties vary, but all specialists agree that it is impossible to apply the technique of the typical treatment at the outset.

Some have advocated treatment in two phases. A first, preanalytic phase, where the therapist can resort to extra-analytic measures, has as its aim the preservation of contact with reality, on the basis of a positive transference, and the development of consciousness of illness and of the wish to be cured. When the schizophrenic becomes more like the neurotic, the second phase can be undertaken. This phase, which is analytic, always takes into consideration the patient's tendency to defend himself against frustration by withdrawal from reality and narcissistic regression.

Other techniques have been suggested; for example, Rosen's "direct analysis" and Sechehaye's symbolic realization, both of which have achieved successful or interesting results. In our opinion, therapeutic research should be economical and should depart from analysis as little as possible. Separating the treatment into two parts rests on an analogy with an already outdated phase of child analysis. An analysis can begin right away, and if need be, the functions of looking after the patient and instructing him can be delegated to a third party. The difficulty is not the lack of transference but the intensity of its results, which can either block the patient with opposition and mutism or flood him through excessive emotion and anxiety, phantasies, delirious ideas and impulsive actions. The measures to take are to avoid producing a transference that it will not be possible to control through psychoanalytic means. This involves a different arrangement of the analytic situation (face to face) and a different management of interpretation (content, formulation, time). The same modifications of the typical treatment may be indicated in serious neurotic conditions, or in severe blocking, when this latter proves impossible to overcome by ordinary methods.

The Psychoanalysis of Criminals

The criminal personality raises particular difficulties for analysis. Some are external difficulties created by the situation; as when these people are being hunted or detained, or are serving a sentence. Intrinsic difficulties created by the criminal personality are even greater. These arise from ego weakness, with numerous immature and egocentric features; from the anomalies of a superego that is often archaic and sadistic; from the fact that relations with others have often developed on a basis of either experienced or inflicted violence; from lack of frankness; from absence of any knowledge of abnormality or desire to be cured; from a disinclination to "return to oneself"; and from instability. Such traits, among others, make criminals unsuitable for the classical form of analytic treatment. In spite of these difficulties there have been enough attempts to give some idea of the modifications necessary here.

Following August Aichhorn, Kurt Eissler has advocated a preanalytic introductory stage with the aim of establishing a positive relation (1950). During this stage, to borrow Anna Freud's expression, the analyst must be anything but a shadow. He should, for example, play the role of an omnipotent and benevolent being. It seems that the delinquent has often experienced in his childhood a disastrous situation, in which he expected help and protection from someone whom he endowed with omnipotence. Later he oscillates between sentiments of omnipotence and of inferiority. Feeling himself at the mercy of a hostile environment that threatens immediate destruction, he escapes panic by aggressive behavior. In the analysis the non-repetition of the traumatic experience leads him to entertain an omnipotent and benevolent idea of the analyst. In other words, he becomes capable of displacing a part of his "omnipotence" onto the analyst, which he could never do with his parents or the authorities.

Eissler also says that the analyst must be capable of surprising the delinquent, must give him satisfaction in the domain of reality the validity of which he accepts (for example, sometimes letting him give people money). We must add that control and calmness must disappoint and frustrate the patient's sado-masochistic aspirations, by refusing him any satisfaction of wishes for inflicted or experienced violence, in any of the many forms in which these aspirations may be expressed.

The expected result of this first stage is, through the development of a positive transference, a decrease in recourse to delinquency and the replacing of aggressiveness by anxiety. The patient, in order to undergo a normal analysis, is then usually passed on to another analyst, since he cannot easily undergo analysis with a person from whom he has received so many satisfactions in the past.

Conclusions

In the treatment of delinquents it is clear that the pre-analytic stage advocated by Eissler, although it takes its inspiration from analysis, still resorts to extra-analytic methods. In the treatment of children a purely analytic technique has been successfully defined. In the psychoses, besides therapeutic situations inaccessible to analysis or any form of psychotherapy, there are cases where analysis develops more favorably than in some neuroses, provided technical conditions do not induce a therapeutic situation where the proper methods of analysis are overthrown. It is therefore permissible to talk of variations of the typical treatment and to distinguish psychoanalytically inspired psychotherapies.

13 / Psychoanalysis and Psychotherapy

Similarities and Differences

Psychotherapy is a treatment that depends on the personal relationship between therapist and patient. Therefore psychoanalysis is a form of psychotherapy. However, it is the custom to distinguish the two. In non-analytic forms of psychotherapy the relationship between patient and psychotherapist is used but not controlled, elucidated and reduced. In analysis the environment and the analyst's role and countertransference are controlled. The analyst confines himself to throwing light on certain unconscious meanings, mainly as regards the transference neurosis. In this way the analyst has the means of knowing and understanding a great deal about the mechanisms of psychotherapy, and numerous findings have been made about the psychic or somatic disorders that make patients resort to psychotherapy. This is why psychoanalysis alone is in a position to produce a theory of psychotherapy, and why various psychotherapeutic methods have tried to use the technical and clinical findings of analysis.

Hypnosis and Suggestion

Psychoanalysis has emerged from hypnosis by passing through the intermediary stages of catharsis and suggestion. Freud had anticipated that the analyst might have to revert to these older methods because of the practical impossibility of applying psychoanalysis to all the patients to be treated. Also, throughout his career Freud never lost his interest in hypnosis and suggestion, especially in order to make the connection between analysis and these techniques precise, notably by discussing the rapport between transference and suggestion. Finally, once his ideas on the structure of the psychic apparatus had matured, Freud developed a theory of hypnosis and suggestion (1921).

Hypnosis may be compared to love. The object, in the form of the hypnotizer, is put in the place of the ego ideal and internalized parental authority is projected upon him. Suggestion does not depend on perception or reasoning but on this erotic link, with the exclusion of all sexual gratification, as distinct from love, where this gratification at least figures in the background as a possible goal. The sense of reality is eliminated and the subject experiences everything the hypnotizer demands and affirms, as in a dream. The hypnotic procedure only serves to fix conscious attention. The subject becomes immersed in an attitude that deprives the world of all interest. His interest becomes concentrated on the hypnotizer, without his being able to account for this, and a transference relationship develops between the two.

Rado (1924) showed that the success of the older methods depended on producing a transference neurosis.

In hypnosis the parent-child relation becomes reactivated. The educative process is repeated by being applied to symptoms of repression brought into force in childhood against instinctual satisfaction. In catharsis the neurosis becomes converted into hysteria and becomes manifest in acute neurotic symptoms. The temporary efficacy of the treatment depends on this conversion.

As Freud anticipated, hypnosis has gained fresh interest, especially in Anglo-Saxon countries (Margaret Brenman, 1947). Under the name *hypnoanalysis* a technique has been tried in which hypnosis is used to explore resistances whose existence is presupposed on an analytic basis. In the intervals between hypnotic sessions "analysis" is carried out and guided by observations made during the hypnotic state. This method can give results in the hands of an experienced psychoanalyst. But it is a non-analytic method, since hypnosis actively induces a parental transference, while the analyst carefully avoids playing the role of the parent that is projected upon him by the patient. As Glover (1939) puts it, hypnoanalysis may perhaps constitute progress in the technique of hypnosis, but it is not such in that of analysis.

The Problem of Short Treatment

The practical interest in shortening analytic treatment is obvious. The *short treatment* consists in applying analytic interpretations to the difficulties and biographical events described by the patient; treatment can be continued for from three to sixty sessions, over a period that may vary from a few days to some months.

The short treatment has produced many successes,

sometimes astonishing ones, but these cannot be relied on firmly. A great deal of ability and attention is needed to develop an effective therapeutic relation and to control it. Short treatment should only be undertaken by competent analysts, and only when, through external circumstances, the usual type of analysis is impossible.

Alexander's analytic therapy is noted for its "rule of flexibility." "Standard" analysis is considered too rigid to be adjusted to all the widely different types of cases. Alexander refers to modifications of the classical technique in the case the treatment of children (Anna Freud, 1926), psychotics and criminals. But he extends the principle of his modifications, the rule of flexibility, to all cases, including adult psychoneuroses and psychosomatic disorders. Psychoanalytic knowledge is such that it allows one to see therapeutic problems from above, "to fly overhead" as it were, and as a result to adopt a "strategic" and not only a tactical attitude. The principal method of analysis is the creation of an atmosphere in which the patient can modify neurotic habits through undergoing a "corrective experience." This result can be more surely, rapidly and intensively obtained if the analyst replaces his spontaneous attitudes (his countertransference, according to Alexander) by consciously assumed attitudes (for example, by playing the role of an understanding father, if the pathogenic parent was authoritarian and hard). Transference must then not only be controlled in its extent and intensity but also, as it were, be provoked. Alexander accuses "standard" analysis of encouraging the patient's dependent needs and so of prolonging the treatment. He wishes to parry this by such measures as the spacing out of sessions and temporary interruptions in treatment, calculated to prevent the patient from becoming too dependent and entrenched.

The changes advocated by Alexander have usually provoked criticism from psychoanalysts. The "rule of flexibility" is a principle not to be contested. It is clear that the treatment is made for the patient and not the other way round. Freud himself recommended flexibility in applying technical "rules." The question is what practical importance to ascribe to this. Most analysts acknowledge that they are not the same with all their patients, the amount of variation being limited by understanding and control of the countertransference. But they are hostile to the principle of playing a part systematically, which can only falsify transference and prevent an analysis of the negative transference. Changes in the rhythm or duration of sessions are extra-analytic measures, even though many analysts have recourse to them (as when spacing out sessions before the final break). But spacing out sessions makes it more difficult to develop and observe the transference; it becomes harder to adjust interpretations; and finally, if the rule of flexibility is understood in this way, it risks making the treatment more planned rather than more flexible, because the interpretations are based on fewer facts and leave less room for hypotheses. As a result, many analysts consider Alexander's changes to be extra-analytic in method, whatever the immediate therapeutic results may be. If changes in technique are indicated in certain categories of cases, it is preferable to reduce these to a minimum, and not to have recourse whenever possible to the one and only interpretation. For Alexander, this is to take too dogmatic a view of analysis; and he does not admit that he goes beyond analysis in making it "a more efficient procedure, a more emotionally significant one and more economic." The shortening of treatment that he gets is only a fortunate result, and not an aim in itself (1950).

Group Psychoanalysis

Group psychotherapy is already of long standing, and the vogue for it dates from World War II. Psychoanalysts consider that it depends on an exploitation of transference. The difference is that group psychotherapy is led by an analyst who, in principle, confines himself to making analytic interpretations.

In the English school efforts have been made to give group psychotherapy a rigorous form. According to Ezriel (1950), each patient brings an unconscious tension connected with an unconscious object to the group, and seeks to discharge this tension by acting upon other members of the group. Group differs from individual analysis in that the other members of the group react instead of confining themselves to listening and interpreting. Because of the complementary nature of the needs, a problem of the communal group always develops; the group is not conscious of it, but it determines group behavior. Each member adopts a particular attitude toward this group tension, and analysis makes it possible to shed light on the particular methods of defense each patient assumes against his dominant unconscious tension. The surest technique is to use only transference interpretations, i.e. interpretations of what is going on in the group "here and now." Certain rigid subjects do not change, others are improved without its being possible to speak of cure in the analytic sense, and in some cases it is possible to observe remarkable and rapid changes.

Even if the therapist's interventions manage to remain analytic, the situation does not, if we consider the absence of "real" rapport and the limitation of expression by action as in a genuine analytic situation. The patient, in contact with a real group, actively expresses his needs in dealings with the other members, who react actively themselves. The production of preconscious material in the presence of several other people by facilitating or inhibiting expression makes for a more direct experience, which encourages anxiety, guilt and shame. In other words, the role of analytic interpretation is diminished at the expense of abreaction.

Group analysis is indicated, like the short treatment, in cases where psychoanalysis is not practicable. It is not indicated for oppositional, inhibited or rigid subjects, who derive no benefit and have a negative effect on the cohesion of the group.

Psychoanalysis and Theatrotherapy

By theatrotherapy is meant a psychotherapeutic technique that uses the improvisation of dramatic scenes on a given theme by a group of either adult or child subjects to present personality or behavioral difficulties in a more or less analogous manner. Psychotherapists usually participate in the dramatic play by orienting and interpreting it. These techniques resemble the psychoanalysis of children through "free" expression in dramatic play and the intervention of action.

Moreno's psychodrama is the best known form of this

therapy (Vienna, 1921; United States, 1926). According to Moreno, the essential element is the actor's freedom of action, which produces spontaneity and is homologous to the rule of free association. The patient chooses his part and those of his supporting cast. The therapist directs the play and then discusses and interprets the enacted scene. A deeper interpretation sees psychodrama not only as expression through action but as symbolic communication (Anzieu).

In France psychoanalysts have worked out a combination of group analysis and psychodrama (Diatkine, Drey-fuss-Moreau, Socarras, Kesteinberg). The sessions are led by two psychoanalysts of different sex, representing the parental couple. The patients choose a theme and allocate the parts. The technical function of the analysts is a subtle one. On the one hand, they must have an animated play, and on the other, they must not enter into the patients' game. Two principles are involved in resolving these contradictory demands. One is to bring the patient to state precisely what it is he expects of the therapist by refusing him, and the other is to do what the patient asks, but so slowly that the situation becomes more and more anxiety-provoking. Interpretations, which are usually given at the end of the session, must neither come too soon nor too late, because if too soon they sterilize dramatic expression, and if too late they allow the patient to escape into the dramatic action and substitute fiction for reality. The principal opposition is from resistances: repetition of scenes that are more and more "real," impoverishment of play, going over to action (in the case of aggressive people), and more and more complex symbolism with a smaller and smaller affective change.

According to Ezriel, it is in the transference analysis, in the analysis of what is going on here and now, that a remedy must be sought. A real group transference does not exist—that is, a transference "of the group" or "upon the group"—but rather there are interferences and resonance between individual transferences. The transference phenomena are concentrated on the analysts with the alternation characteristic of this type of therapy. The psychoanalysts form a group representing the parental structure, which produces ways of being infantile and presocial in the patients, and corresponds to the archaic organization of the neurosis. The links that unite the patients are those of their illness and of their communal situation in relation to the therapists.

Psychotherapy under Narcosis

By narcoanalysis is meant a therapeutic procedure the aim of which is to produce a kind of accelerated or rough and ready psychoanalysis. The introduction of a drug into the organism, by removing certain controls, allows the externalization of tendencies, emotions and memories that would not otherwise manifest themselves.

In one sense, the technique is as old as the world, and the wisdom of the people of all nations has enshrined it in the adage *in vino veritas.* During World War II it was used by American doctors to resolve traumatic neuroses induced by combat.

The aim is to reach the deepest preconscious levels and to free emotions that are motivating defense. In the intervals between narcotic treatment psychotherapy is pursued, on the basis of indications collected from the former. The introduction of drugs into the organism, whether by the psychotherapist or by another, does not allow the creation of a psychoanalytic situation. The shedding of light on resistance and transference is even more compromised than in hypnoanalysis. To use Glover's expression, it becomes a question of "controlled narcotherapy." This method gives results in cases where neurosis is the result of traumata, where emotional shock has reactivated infantile traumata and defenses have become mobilized to a pathological degree. In all other cases, it amounts merely to exploration under very artificial conditions, and the results obtained cannot be used by psychoanalysis, for the analysis of the ego and its defenses must still be carried out. Often "narcoanalysts" are not psychoanalysts.

14 / Psychoanalytic Research

Psychoanalysis as "Action-Research"

In psychoanalytic treatment investigation is inseparable from treatment. This does not mean that analysis is an investigative treatment. Progress in knowledge of the self is at once a means, a sign and a consolidation of changes, accomplished through a lived experience, the relation with the analyst. The analyst's role is therapeutic, and from this point of view investigation is only a method, scientific results only by-products, whatever their interest, importance or value. Scientifically, psychoanalysis is not "pure research" but "action-research."

The Psychoanalytic Field

Seen from outside, the psychoanalytic method has analogies with the experimental method. In order to let the transference develop in all its purity, analysis takes place in artificial conditions, controlled and uniform. The frequency, duration and timing of the sessions remain constant; the environment, the role and attitude of the analyst change as little as possible; and under these conditions the introduction of an interpretation may be compared to that of an independent variable, the effects of which may be followed out. But this is only an ideal. Changes may be produced accidentally. In general, the patient reacts to these in the context of his dominant tendencies of the moment; for example, by interpreting them as tests introduced by the analyst. Such accidents also occur in research.

The comparison may be taken further. Refinement in psychological experimentation has led to taking into consideration factors long considered negligible: for example, the environment of the experimental animal and the personality of the experimenter. Psychoanalysis has probably played its part in such preoccupations. In psychoanalysis the part played by countertransference was early recognized, that is, the fact that the analyst is not confined to listening and interpreting but also has personal reactions, which are not only intellectual but also emotional, not only conscious but also preconscious and unconscious. Countertransference is inevitable and is not a technical fault; it can reveal something about the patient's correlated dispositions. The fault is in misunderstanding it, or in acting it out. Hence the necessity for controlling it, by the analysis of the psychoanalyst, followed by autoanalysis. Not much work has yet been done on countertransference, and this is one of the directions technical research should take. Its importance lies in a conception of the psychoanalytic field other than as a field of observation where the analyst has the standing of a non-participating observer, and by defining it as "the field of interaction between the psychoanalysand and the psychoanalyst."

Analytic Material

The fundamental rule draws attention to the verbal expression of freely associated ideas, that is, to everything the patient thinks and feels, without voluntarily choosing or excluding anything. An involuntary and unconscious control becomes substituted for the voluntary and conscious control and is the principal objective of analytic observation. The patient talks about his symptoms and difficulties, his memories, his future, his present life, his dreams, his treatment, his relation with the analyst. The choice and the unconscious links between the themes are only part of the material. The style, tone of voice, and method of expression mingle with the words; emotional expression is added to the verbal, as are also postural attitudes and gestures, visceral reactions and impressions, and actions unachieved or accomplished before, during and after the sessions. This leads us to say that the psychoanalytic material is the behavior of the analysand, taking behavior to mean the totality of his relations and communications with his environment, of which the privileged section is what happens during the session.

Associations of ideas make for ways of approach and symbolic flights that are linked to the relation of patient and analyst.

The Genesis of Interpretation

Interpretation is the psychoanalytic act *par excellence*. At whatever moment of the investigation, it consists in a discovery by the analyst of the meaning of the material, that is, of the property through which the patient's acts have the sense of reducing his tensions and expressing his potentialities. If, for example, a male patient in addressing a male analyst speaks of a "man to man" relation, and after a while adds "or between a woman and a man," it seems that he has expressed, while trying to repudiate it, the homosexual implications of his first phrase. In general, an interpretation consists in applying certain known relations, which play the parts of rules, to concrete data. It is the same in psychoanalysis: the concrete data is the "psychoanalytic material," and the rules of interpretation are derived from the psychological knowledge the analyst has drawn from his life experience and culture, his own analysis, his psychoanalytic studies and the analyses he has already carried out.

The relative parts that intuition and reason play in this have been discussed. For some, analytic interpretation comes from the analyst's unconscious, from his identification with the patient, from a "third ear" (Reik); for others, the role of logic, reason and strategy, as well as of tactics, is more important (Reich).

This discussion seems outdated (Kris). Partly it depends on the situation: sometimes interpretation can emerge spontaneously through the association of ideas, either progressively or abruptly, thanks to some detail; at other times procedure is more discursive, as through linking one session to the next, systematically. It also depends on the psychoanalyst's "personal equation." In general, progress in knowledge has increased the possibility of conjecture, but in the immediate work of analysis the role of preconscious processes remains considerable; they are the source of certain interpretations that gush forth and guarantee the analyst's spontaneity. These also intervene in the formulation of interpretations: a change of word, the choice of the mode of judgment, can make a correct interpretation acceptable. Countertransference must not be neglected; it is not enough to keep it in mind and control it. An emotional reaction can give the analyst information on the patient's attitude: if the therapist feels disappointed to see his efforts unappreciated, there is a chance that the patient neither wishes to recognize them nor to accept them.

The Validity of Interpretations

According to a widespread prejudice, the analytic method of investigation labels the patient's communications with ready-made formulae. This prejudice has no justification in fact. Like all interpretation, analytic interpretation applies connections extracted from a body of "knowledge" to facts, but it applies these in a specific manner. A general interpretation has no therapeutic force or logical value. Furthermore, a stereotyped application of already known connections would not permit the discovery of new ones, whereas these are discovered. Finally, the establishment of the proof is submitted to certain criteria that psychoanalysis shares with clinical investigation. The degree of certainty is a function of the richness and variety of the data (the criterion of sufficient information); of the relationship between the data and the given complete person, considered throughout his history and in the totality of his rapport with his environment (the criterion of the internal coherence of the hypothesis); and finally, of the most probable interpretation—that which takes in the maximum of facts and involves the minimum of hypothesis (the criterion of economy). The analytic method differs from the clinical insofar as interpretation intervenes in the manner of an independent variable in the development of the analytic situation, and it is to this development that more specific criteria belong. A radically false interpretation, besides being difficult to make, leaves the patient quite indifferent or has only the effect of a suggestion in relation to the transference.

More often the interpretation is incorrect because it is partial. The classical example is an interpretation that directly lights up an unconscious tendency while ignoring the transformations of this tendency through ego defense and the relation with reality. Such an interpretation can arouse severe anxiety and repression. Criteria for correct interpretations have been minutely itemized by various authors (Susan Isaacs, 1939). They can be summarized by saying that an adequate interpretation produces positive effects in the patient's behavior under analysis. There is a decrease in anxiety and in defenses connected with the problem in question, a bringing to light of fresh facts, a correction in the transference projections upon the analyst, an emergence of new problems connected with the preceding ones, and renewed anxiety and resistance.

These principles are as valid for interpretations bearing on the present as for "reconstructions" bearing on the past. With regard to facts that more particularly concern the past, the analyst's inferences can sometimes be confirmed by external proof. We can equally well point to their conformity with what we know in general of the laws of the development of individual differences.

15 / Psychoanalysis and the Humanities

Psychoanalysis is unique among the medical disciplines in having extensive connections with the social sciences and in playing no less an important part there than in psychiatry (Freud, 1922). Part of Freud's work was devoted to "applied psychoanalysis," and today this represents about a fifth of all psychoanalytic output. The field is even more extensive if we take into account both the direct and the indirect influence of psychoanalysis. Although psychoanalysis can be applied in a non-medical way (as in education), applied psychoanalysis consists principally in the application of analytic conceptions to the social sciences, in the absence of analytic investigation properly speaking and of all the material furnished by a psychoanalysis.

Freud himself applied psychoanalytic theory to literature, art, religion, mythology, folklore and sociology. In *Totem and Taboo* he reconstructed the origins of social life and religion in the light of the Oedipus complex. One day the band of brothers, ambivalent in their feelings toward their father (admiring and hating him simultaneously), rose up in revolt and defeated him. Prohibition against the murder of the totem derives from their guilt and their need to become reconciled with the father; incest prohibition neutralized the fraternal sexual rivalry and fratricidal tendencies. But the brothers' inner attitude toward the father remained ambivalent, and the institution of the totemic feast was to commemorate their former victory over him. Thus recourse to the Oedipus complex allows us to explain at the same time the cult of the totem and exogamy.

R. de Saussure has studied the application of psychoanalysis to history and especially to the "Greek miracle."

Literary or artistic work can be interpreted directly by an intuitive method that makes use of a knowledge of symbols. It is possible to some extent to study the genesis of a work of art in connection with the artist's personality, although difficulties arise because biographical data cannot completely replace the actual living facts. Such research does not imply that the work of art must be viewed as an illness or an attempt at cure; in recent years, under the influence of ego analysis, the view of art as self-expression has receded in favor of the view of it as adaptation. At the same time more stress is now laid on the social aspects, particularly the function of communication (Kris).

The interpretation of religious phenomena, especially those based on the Judaeo-Christian tradition, centers on Oedipal conflict. Freud's views center on the nature of the relation with the father. More recently, interest has been aroused by the relation with the mother. Various rites, especially initiation rites, dramatize Oedipal problems and various magical methods for escaping the fear of death.

Research on myths and folklore has used analytic

theory more than it has sought to establish its validity. Classical theories, such as those of the impulses and the Oedipus complex, have been used most. The universality and ubiquity of myths have been linked with a biological factor—the long dependence of the human infant. The myth is an attempt to resolve a current anxiety-producing situation by placing it in the past (Roheim). Many works have also emphasized the role of the pre-Oedipal mother and the anxious fascination over a cruel mother who devours her children. Despite its instinctual roots myth becomes modified along with historical changes.

Psychoanalytic influence has also affected cultural anthropology. For example, the way children are reared has become a chief method of approach in studying particular cultures. But cultural anthropology has not confined itself to the use of analytic theory; it has also limited and modified various concepts, for example, that of the universality of the latency period. The most famous controversies have taken place over the universality of the Oedipus complex, which was supported by Freud, criticized by Malinowski (using data collected on matriarchal societies), and taken up again by Roheim, who linked it with a universal biological fact: that we wish to be adults when we are children, and children when we are adults.

The application of psychoanalytic theory is more difficult as regards sociology, mainly on account of the statistical and impersonal nature of the data. But analytic influence has been considerable in spite of this: especially in social psychology, with its research on the socialization of the individual, group behavior, the dynamics of the group, and certain collective phenomena. This has been facilitated by the development of ego psychology and a clearer sense of the specificity of problems, for example, in industrial psychology.

Another current can also be discerned: one in which problems of interest to psychoanalysis—such as identification and the social role—have been envisaged in sociological terms. Many important works have analyzed the effects of cultural and social factors on psychoanalytic treatment, and although no fundamental changes have resulted, interesting refinements have been introduced.

The application of psychoanalysis to psychological and social research produces methodological problems.

The use of analytic concepts does not imply a reduction of everything to psychopathological terms, or a devaluation of the life and work of man. Dream analysis shows that mechanisms reputed to be pathogenic occur equally in the well-adapted individual (Freud).

Psychological interrelations discovered in the individual case cannot be transposed to the level of groups and collectivities, but the circumstances of a discovery are not always decisive as to its nature. There is an astonishing convergence between the discoveries of Freud and Abraham on mourning and the research work of Robert Hertz on the representation of death among primitive societies (Lagache, 1938). Also, the technique and theory of psychoanalysis are quite opposed to a psychology of the isolated man.

The truth is that the transposition of an analytic concept is without intrinsic value. Psychoanalysis can furnish a working hypothesis, but its verification depends on the data and methods proper to the field in which the hypothesis is applied. Furthermore, the proposed explanation is not in principle exhaustive, and must be articulated with independent factors, which may be biological, historical, sociological, economic, cultural and so on. Applied psychoanalysis requires a double competence—familiarity with analysis and with the field of application—which leads us to say that the analyst who plays sociologist and the art critic who plays analyst are in the same boat.

It is easy enough to understand why psychoanalysis has the power to expand and to penetrate into the arts and social sciences. Psychoanalytic material brings into play the whole person, the full course of his history, the totality of his rapports with his environment, and the diversity of his object relations. The whole technique, the conception of the personality, its history, its structure, its behavior: all constantly have reference to interpersonal relations. Above all, psychoanalysis is practically the only technique for studying unconscious processes. The fertility of psychoanalytic theory was renewed when, passing beyond the depth psychology of the impulses, it supplemented it with ego psychology and the mechanisms of defense. Recent developments in the theory of object relations and communication are producing an approach increasingly adequate for applied psychoanalytic research.

16 / Psychoanalysis and Morals

Moral norms and values are part of social reality. Insofar as it is an anthropological discipline, psychoanalysis encounters these. During treatment the psychoanalyst is concerned with patients who are involved in moral problems and neurotic guilt. Sublimation is considered to be a fortunate result of unconscious conflict. All this raises the question of the connection between psychoanalysis and morals. Psychoanalysis has been accused by some of amorality and of not completing treatment with a moralizing effect. Others have reproached it with concealing an occult morality. Such speculations are echoed in the claims of patients, who often ask the psychoanalyst for punishments or rewards, praise or blame.

The accusation of immorality rests on a misconception. For one, the psychoanalyst must preserve a receptive attitude, free from blame, in the face of all the patient's manifestations. Secondly, interpretation is calculated to reduce ego defense and neurotic guilt. And thirdly, a certain liberation of sexual and aggressive tendencies is part of the therapeutic goal. In this way sometimes the mistaken idea arises that analysis must free all manner of guilt and allow one to do exactly as one pleases.

In fact, there is room for a distinction between neurotic guilt and guilt based on reality. Unruly behavior and license show the subject's alienation in a narcissistic ideal of omnipotence. With man, adjustment to reality rests with the ego and not with the impulses. Within the treatment license in behavior is resistance through action that deflects the subject from the true goal, which is conquest of inner freedom; it is the opposite of genuine liberty. And it is one of the occasions on which the analyst may and should bring the rule of abstinence into play; such an intervention is therapeutic and not moral.

It is no less true that a certain value system is immanent in psychoanalytic treatment, as in all human work, including the search for scientific truth. A common search for truth is one of the incentives of the treatment—a fundamental rule that makes the patient's sincerity an initial condition. The treatment also implies a certain conception of mental health, the elimination of the restraints of the id and the superego, and the promotion, through a strengthening of the ego, of reason and judgment. In connection with the social environment, all this means that neither an exaggerated conformity nor an exuberance of destructive tendencies is the norm. We may suppose that the normal functioning of the personality requires compromise between society's conserving and creative forces. Thus to acknowledge reality and adjust oneself to it does not mean that one must accept it passively and give up trying to alter it.

Without the psychoanalyst becoming transformed into a preacher, psychoanalytic treatment is in many respects a "moral experience" that teaches both the art of living and wisdom.

17 / The Psychoanalyst

Psychoanalysis is an art concerned with understanding and modifying irrational phenomena, but it is a rational art, founded on positive knowledge. Each psychoanalysis is always a research, but discovery does not spring *ex nihilo*, nor out of the shadows of the unconscious. Interpretation often develops through progressive gropings. Even if it is invested with the spontaneous allure of intuition, it is in reality the application of a general knowledge to a particular, concrete situation. The psychoanalyst is neither a diviner nor a wizard.

The necessity for a scientific education is beyond discussion. The psychoanalyst cannot improvise his part. Although he is a doctor, a psychiatrist and a psychologist, sometimes misadventures due to autodidacticism occur, when specialist knowledge is lacking in psychoanalytic theory (clinical, technical or applied), knowledge that must be practical as well as rational, and that helps to control the beginner's first analyses. However, a psychiatric, psychological and psychoanalytic education is still too narrow if it is not supported by a culture that brings in the humanities and experience of life.

The strict formation of a specialist must surpass such necessities. A scientific education, although necessary, is not sufficient to produce a psychoanalyst. This is because the link between art and science is very much in question here, and because certain implications of the art of medicine are pushed here to their ultimate logical consequences. The therapeutic interrelation is the therapeutic agent, as Freud discovered in converting the obstacles of resistance and transference into instruments of treatment. The accent placed today on the technical role of the analyst and the countertransference reveals even more the nature of analysis as a process of interaction and communication. And so not only the intelligence and knowledge of the psychoanalyst are brought into play, but his whole personality.

It is curious that despite the number of analysts who have undergone personal analysis we know little about the analyst's personality, and certainly do not have a coordinated body of knowledge. We can imagine that a research program would probably show a considerable diversity of human types. If this is a correct hypothesis, it implies significant differences in the manner of conducting an analysis, without, however, invalidating the whole process: the same ends can be attained by widely different methods, and diversity in the type of patient suggests in itself a certain diversity of needs. It is also likely that—even more than the relative uniformity of education—prolonged involvement in the same activity and submission to the same situations and tensions tend to make men of different origins more uniform. Factorial research has shown that extent of experience links psychotherapists more closely than similarity of education or sharing of doctrine.

Since there is a lack of empirical data, one can only speculate. What does the practice of analysis require? Certainly we must mention a receptive attitude to the patient, the creation of a favorable atmosphere for his communications (or at least of one that is not unfavorable), and patience until the full meaning of his talk emerges. This implies the suspension of personal answers and the silencing of the desires, emotions and beliefs possessed by the analyst. This is a suspension, not a blocking and a misconception, since the only way of neutralizing their interference and exploiting their indications is to acknowledge them.

As in most psychological work, the selection of psychoanalytic candidates is by the clinical method. The candidate has an interview with two or more analysts, who compare their observations and opinions. Each conducts his own examination as he pleases. It is usually easy to get agreement on certain points, such as cultural background, scientific education and professional qualifications. Other aspects involve a more subtle examination: the capacity for communication, maturity of character and judgment, and success in private life. As a whole, the criteria for mental health are applied, as psychoanalysis conceives these. Reservations are also made regarding individuals of too perfect balance, the reasons for which are often strong defenses and affecting inhibitions. The presence of neurotic difficulties does not eliminate a candidate, provided these are not too pronounced and the elucidation and integration of underlying conflicts can reasonably be predicted. Nor is the experience of such difficulties (which so often motivates the choice of a psychological vocation) considered to be without value. In principle, the choice of a candidate only implies a trial, the result of which will show whether the choice was well founded.

A didactic analysis is the main element in psychoanalytic training: the apprentice-analyst undergoes a prolonged and deep analysis carried out in the usual spirit and with the usual technique. Only a personal analysis can free the judgment from the misconceptions and distortions that unknown and unresolved unconscious conflicts impose upon it. This alone prevents the psychoanalyst from letting his personal motivations, and especially his self-esteem, interfere with his analytic interventions.

(And even if the didactic analysis is long and deep, this does not absolve the analyst from frequently turning in upon himself. The periodic resumption of the personal analysis, which was recommended by Freud but is rarely practiced, would be even more fertile after several years of analytic practice, by which time the analyst better feels the need and importance of it.)

The work of analysis also exacts a knowledge of the art of living. It constantly imposes suspensions, restrictions and canalization in the potential for response and personal expression. It is desirable for the arrangement of the analyst's time to allow him change of activity and periods of rest and vacation. It is absolutely necessary that he not have to seek in his work for the security and satisfaction he cannot find in his life.

Bibliography

Abraham, Karl. *Clinical Essays and Papers on Psychoanalysis*, ed. Hilda Abraham and D. R. Ellison. New York: Basic Books, 1956.

Fenichel, Otto. *Collected Papers*, ed. Hannah Fenichel and David Rapaport. 2 vols. New York: W. W. Norton, 1953.

Ferenczi, Sandor. *First Contributions to Psychoanalysis*, tr. Ernest Jones. London: Hogarth Press, 1952.

Freud, Anna. *The Ego and the Mechanisms of Defense*. New York: International Universities Press, 1957.

———. *The Psychoanalytical Treatment of Children*. New York: International Universities Press, 1960.

Freud, Sigmund. *An Autobiographical Study*, tr. James Strachey. New York: W. W. Norton, 1952.

———. *Collected Papers*, ed. Ernest Jones. 5 vols. New York: Basic Books, 1959.

———. *The Complete Psychological Works*. Standard Edition. 24 vols. New York: Macmillan.

———. *Group Psychology and the Analysis of the Ego*. New York: Bantam Books. (Paperback.)

———. *The Interpretation of Dreams*. New York: Modern Library.

————. *New Introductory Lectures on Psychoanalysis.* New York: W. W. Norton, 1933.

————. *The Origins of Psychoanalysis: Sigmund Freud's Letters, Drafts and Notes to Wilhelm Fliess,* ed. Anna Freud and others. New York: Doubleday & Co., 1957. (Paperback.)

————. *The Psychopathology of Everyday Life.* New York: New American Library, 1952. (Paperback.)

————. *Three Essays on the Theory of Sexuality.* New York: Hillary House Publishers.

————. *Totem and Taboo.* New York: Vintage Books. (Paperback.)

————. *Wit and Its Relation to the Unconscious.* New York: Dodd, Mead & Co., 1916 (?).

———— with Joseph Breuer. *Studies in Hysteria.* Boston: Beacon Press, 1958. (Paperback.)

Jones, Ernest. *Essays in Applied Psychoanalysis.* 2 vols. London: Hogarth Press, 1951.

————. *The Life and Work of Sigmund Freud,* ed. Lionel Trilling and Steven Marcus. New York: Basic Books, 1961.

Klein, Melanie. *Contributions to Psychoanalysis: 1921–1945.* New York: Hillary House Publishers.

————. *The Psychoanalysis of Children.* New York: Grove Press, 1960. (Paperback.)

————. and others. *Developments in Psychoanalysis.* New York: Hillary House Publishers.

Sachs, Hanns. *Freud: Master and Friend.* Cambridge: Harvard University Press, 1944.

Index

Abraham, Karl, 10, 13, 32, 71, 75, 76, 77, 134
Abreaction, 107
Abstinence, rule of, 108
"Acting out," 52
Action-research, psychoanalysis as, 125
Adler, Alfred, 11
Aggression, 11, 13, 15, 16, 28, 75–76
Agoraphobia, 68
Aichhorn, August, 84, 113
Alexander, Franz, 84, 90, 91, 94, 97, 118, 119
Alloplastic behavior, 45, 49
Allport, Gordon W., 34
Ambivalence, 11, 30, 63, 64
Amentia, 75
Anal-sadistic stage, 30
Analyst, qualifications of, 139–142
  role of, in treatment, 100–101
Anger, 15, 16, 56, 61
Anthropology, cultural, 133
Anxiety, 26, 38, 43, 44, 46, 62, 64, 68, 70
  castration, 13, 31, 80, 81, 82

Art, 21, 131, 132, 135
Autoerotic satisfaction, 29
Automatic writing, 6
Autoplastic behavior, 45
Aversion, 43–44

Behavior, 42–50
  alloplastic, 45, 49
  autoplastic, 45
  and communication, 49–50
  criminal, 84–86
  de-differentiation of, 78
  defined, 42–43
  elaboration of, 44
  integration as goal of, 46, 66
  and motivation, 43–44
  primitivation of, 78
  secondary effects of, 48
Behavioral disorders, functional conception of, 65–67
Behaviorism, 24
Bernheim, Hippolyte, 5, 7, 8
Beyond the Pleasure Principle (Freud), 11
Biting, in childhood, 29–30
Bleuler, Eugen, 10, 77

Blum, Gerald, 41
Bowlby, John, 84, 85
Brenman, Margaret, 117
Breuer, Joseph, 3, 4, 5, 7
Brucke's Laboratory, 6
Brunswick, Ruth Mack, 32

Cannon, Walter B., 24, 89, 90
Castration anxiety, 13, 31, 80, 81, 82
Catalepsy, 5
Catatonic symptoms, 78
Catharsis, under hypnosis, 5, 6, 7, 8, 116, 117
Censor, 12, 35, 58
Character neuroses, 82–83
Charcot, Jean-Martin, 5, 7
Chicago School, 91, 94
Childhood, impulse and object stages during, 29–31
    unstable affective relations in, and criminal behavior, 85–86
Children, psychoanalysis of, 109–111
Claustrophobia, 68
Coitus interruptus, 69
Collective unconscious, 11, 40
Communication, and behavior, 49–50
Compulsions, 68
Condensation, in dreams, 57
Conflict, between id and ego, 26, 74
    between ego and reality, 74
    mental phenomena described in terms of, 15ff., 66
    between needs for dependence and for independence, 83
    during phallic stage, 31
    See also Neurosis; Oedipus complex; Psychosis
Consciousness, 9, 12, 35, 48, 49, 50

Constancy, principle of, 18–19, 24, 28, 43
Conversion hysteria, 70, 89–90
Countertransference, 100, 126, 129
Criminals, behavior of, 84–86
    psychoanalysis of, 112–114
Cultural anthropology, 133

Daydreams, 70
Death impulses, 11, 12, 22, 27
Defense mechanisms, 12, 14, 47, 58, 96
Defense motives, 44
Demand, defined, 43
Dementia praecox, 77
Denial, as defense mechanism, 47
Depression, 17, 68, 76, 81
Desire, defined, 43
Didactic analysis, in psychoanalytic training, 142
Dipsomania, 80, 81, 82
Displacement, in dreams, 57
Dissociative adjustment, 66
Distaste, 44, 46
Dramatization, in dreams, 57, 58
Dream(s), 6, 35, 56–64
    elaboration of, 57
    as guardian of sleep, 56, 60, 64
    interpretation of, 58–64
    mechanisms of, 57
    painful, 60–64
    regression in, 62
    repressed emotions in, 47, 58, 62, 64
    theory of, 16, 56–64
    as wish fulfillment, 56, 60, 64
Dream screen, 59
Drug addiction, 80
Dynamic perspective, in psychoanalysis, 15, 16, 17

Economic perspective, in psycho-analysis, 15–16
Effect, law of, 24
Ego, 10, 12, 13, 14, 16, 21, 33, 36–41 *passim*, 44, 45, 46, 47, 96, 105
    of the criminal, 112
    in neurosis, 26, 67, 70, 73
    in psychosis, 74, 78
    in sleep and dreams, 55–64 *passim*
Ego and the Id, The (Freud), 36
Ego impulses, 26, 27
Ego strength, 44, 67, 137
Eissler, Kurt, 113, 114
Electroshock therapy, 75
Emotions, defenses against, 47
    motivation manifested through, 43, 44
Epilepsy, 97
Erogenous zones, 29
Eros (life impulses), 11, 12, 27
Exterofective mechanisms, 88, 90

Fechner, Gustav, 18, 24
Fenichel, Otto, 23, 47, 62, 90, 91, 93
    quoted, 83
Ferenczi, Sandor, 10, 50, 93
Fetishism, 80
Fixation, 31, 45, 71, 73, 74, 77, 79, 102
    anal-sadistic, 17, 79
    Oedipal, 72
    oral, 17, 76, 81
Folklore, 131, 132
Free association, 8, 99–100, 127
Frequency, principle of, 24
Freud, Anna, 14, 39, 47, 96, 109, 110, 113, 118
Freud, Sigmund, 3, 5, 6–7, 13, 18, 25–26, 92, 95, 106, 108, 119, 131, 133, 134, 142
    on analyst's role in treatment, 100
    on consciousness, 48–49
    on delusion of persecution, 78–79
    dream theory of, 16, 56–58, 61
    first theories of, 9–10, 34–36
    on hypnosis, 8, 116, 117
    metapsychology of, 15, 16–17
    on mourning, 76, 134
    on neurosis, 69–70, 72, 75
    on psychic apparatus, 34–39
    psychoanalysis invented by, 7–9
    on psychosis, 74, 75, 111
    quoted, 104
    on sleep, 55
    on slips and errors in everyday life, 53–54
    thought, theory of, formulated by, 45
Friedlander, Kate, 84
Frustration, 11, 22, 72, 74, 78, 80, 92, 102, 103, 105

Gastric neurosis, 91
Genital stage, 31
Glover, Edward, 117, 124
Groddeck, Georg W., 37
Group psychoanalysis, 120–121, 122
Guilt, 26, 44, 46, 58, 61, 68, 76, 80, 84, 135, 137

Healy, William, 84
Hebephrenic symptoms, 78
Hertz, Robert, 134
Histology of the Nervous System (Freud), 6
Homeostasis, 24
Homosexuality, 67, 77, 79, 80, 81
Horney, Karen, 14
Humanities, and psychoanalysis, 131–135

Hypertension, 90, 93
Hypnoanalysis, 117
Hypnosis, 7
  catharsis under, 5, 6, 7, 8, 116, 117
  Freud's views on, 8, 116, 117
  and hysteria, 5, 7, 117
  as research method, 6
  stages of, described by Charcot, 5
  and suggestion, 116–117
  therapeutic effect of, 6 ⏝
Hysteria, 6, 7, 72
  anxiety, with phobias, 70
  conversion, 70, 89–90
  and hypnosis, 5, 7, 117

Id, 12, 16, 36, 37, 39, 74, 78, 105, 137
Imago, 46
Impulse stages, 29, 40
Impulses, aggressive, 11, 13, 15, 16, 28
  death, 11, 12, 22, 27
  defined, 25–26
  disintegrations of, 28
  education of, 32–33
  ego, 26, 27
  first theory of, 26–27
  fixation of, 31
  life, 11, 12, 27
  maturation of, 28–32
  second theory of, 27–28
  sexual, 11, 13, 15, 26
  transformation of, 16
Incest, 61, 70
Infantile neurosis, 71, 103
Infantile sexuality, 80, 81
Inhibition, Symptom and Anxiety (Freud), 13
Initial interview, 96–98
Insomnia, 55–56, 68
Instinct, 25

Integration, as goal of behavior, 46, 66
Interofective mechanisms, 88, 90
Interpretation, genesis of, 127–129
  validity of, 129–130
Interpretation of Dreams, The (Freud), 9, 34, 58, 59
Interview, initial, 96–98
Introduction to Narcissism (Freud), 10-11
Isaacs, Susan, 130

Janet, Pierre, 5, 6, 19
Jaspers, Karl, 77, 78
Jones, Ernest, 6, 10
Jung, C. G., 10, 11, 40, 77

Klein, Melanie, 13, 32, 72, 109, 110
Knight, R. P., 106
Kraepelin, Emil, 77
Kris, Ernst, 17, 128, 132

Lagache, Daniel, 76, 79, 134
Latency period, 31, 40
Law of effect, 24
Learning processes, 24, 33, 35, 67, 85
Lethargy, as stage of hypnosis, 5
Lewin, Bertram D., 59
Libido, 11, 21, 26, 27, 28
Liébault, A.-A., 7
Life impulses, 11, 12, 27
Low, Barbara, 18

Malinowski, Bronislaw, 133
Manic-depressive psychosis, 31, 75
Masochism, 12, 33, 61, 80
  moral, 38, 39, 44, 46, 60, 61
Masturbation, 56

Melancholia, 11, 12, 16, 38, 75, 76
Mental illness, functional conception of, 65–67
Metapsychology, 15, 16–17
Meynert, Theodore, 75
Minimum, rule of, 108
Moebius, Paul J., 5
Morals, and psychoanalysis, 136–138
Moreno, J. L., 121, 122
Motivation, 43–44
Mourning, 76, 134
Mythology, 131, 132, 133

Nancy school, 5, 7
Narcissism, 16, 26–27, 30, 38, 111
Narcoanalysis, 123–124
Needs, motivation manifested through, 43
Neurosis, 14, 17, 26, 32
    cardiac, 92
    cause of, 71–72
    character, 82–83
    of destiny, 11, 22, 48, 52
    gastric, 91
    impulsive, 81
    infantile, 71, 103
    obsessional, 11, 17, 32, 38, 60, 68, 70, 73
    organic, 92
    transference, 67, 101–104
    traumatic, 11, 12, 61, 68–69
    vegetative, 90–92
    See also Psychoneuroses
Neurosurgery, 75
Nietzsche, Friedrich, 37
Nightmare, 62, 64
Nunberg, Hermann, 38

Object relations, 17, 45–46, 50, 72
Object stages, 29

Obsession, 11, 17, 32, 38, 60, 68, 70, 73
Oedipus complex, 10, 12, 30–31, 38, 40, 72, 80, 97, 110, 131, 132, 133
Oral satisfaction, 29
Organic processes, and personality, 88–89
    psychology of, 74–75
Osler, William, quoted, 87
Overdetermination, in dreams, 57

Paralysis, general, psychology of, 75
    hysterical, 5
Paranoia, 12, 78
Penis envy, 13, 31
Peptic ulcer, 91, 92
Persecution, delusion of, 78–79
Personality, 34
    genesis of, 39–41
    related to organism, 88
    psychoneuroses, role in, 71
    See also Psychic apparatus
Perversions, 80–82
Phallic stage, 30–31
Pity, 82
Pleasure-unpleasure principle, 18, 19, 35, 105
Preconscious, 12, 16, 35, 36
Progression, 17
Projection, 52, 79
    defined, 49
Psychic apparatus, 11, 12, 16, 18
    first theory of, 34–36
    second theory of, 36–39
    See also Personality
Psychic Mechanism of Hysterical Phenomena, The (Freud), 7
Psychodrama, 121–122
Psychological Automatism (Janet), 5

Psychoneuroses, 67–68, 70–71
    cause of, 71–72
    classification of, 68–71
    symptoms of, formation of, 72–74
    See also Neurosis
Psychopathology of Everyday Life, The (Freud), 9
Psychosis, 17, 74–80
    functional, 74
    manic-depressive, 31, 75
    paranoid, 12, 78
    predisposition to, 75–77
    psychoanalysis of, 111–112
Psychosomatic medicine, 87
Psychotherapy, group, 120–121
    under narcosis, 123–124
    psychoanalysis as form of, 115–124
    See also Treatment, psychoanalytic
Puberty, 16, 28, 77

Rado, S., 116
Rapaport, David, 45
Rationalization, 52
    defined, 49
Reaction formation, 32, 47
Reality principle, 19–21, 24, 35, 105
Regression, 17, 31, 62, 73, 74, 77, 80, 102, 111
Reich, Wilhelm, 128
Reik, Theodore, 84, 128
Religion, 11, 21, 131, 132
Repetition compulsion, 11, 18, 21–24, 39, 44, 52, 105
Repression, 9–10, 12, 16, 19, 21, 26, 47, 58, 62, 64, 73
Research, psychoanalytic, 125–130
Resistance, 10, 11, 96, 140

Restitutive tendency, in repetition compulsion, 23
Retroactive undoing, 47
Róheim, Géza, 133
Rosen, J. N., 111

Sachs, Hanns, 6
Sadism, 12, 17, 30, 33, 80
Salpêtrière school, 5
Saussure, R. de, 132
Schilder, Paul, 75
Schizophrenia, 75, 77, 78, 97, 111
Schreber, Daniel Paul, 78
Sechehaye, M. A., 111
Secondary elaboration, in dreams, 57, 59
Sexual impulses, 11, 13, 15, 26
Shame, 44, 46, 91
Sleep, 55, 56, 62
    guarded by dreams, 56, 60, 64
Slips, Freudian, 53–54
Sociology, 131, 133–134, 135
Somatic disorders, 74–75, 87–94
Somnambulism, as stage of hypnosis, 5, 6
Staub, Hugo, 84
Structural perspective, psychoanalytic, 15, 16, 17
Studies in Hysteria (Breuer and Freud), 3, 7, 9, 95
Sublimation, 33, 45, 48, 136
Sucking, in childhood, 29
Suggestion, 7, 8
    and hypnosis, 116–117
    therapeutic effect of, 6
Suicide, 76, 77
Superego, 12, 16, 36, 38–39, 41, 44, 79, 85, 105, 110, 112, 137
Symbolization, in dreams, 57

Teething, 29, 30
Thanatos (death impulses), 11, 12, 22, 27

Theatrotherapy, 121–123
Theft, 86
Three Contributions to the Theory of Sex (Freud), 9
Toilet training, 30, 32
Tolman, Edward C., 24
Topographical approach, in psychoanalytic treatment, 96
Totem and Taboo (Freud), 131
Toxicomania, 81
Transference, 5, 9, 10, 11, 22, 67, 101–104, 111, 114, 120, 123, 140
Traumatic neurosis, 11, 12, 61, 68–69
Treatment, psychoanalytic, 95–107
  analyst's role in, 100–101
  of children, 109–111
  of criminals, 112–114
  external conditions for, 98–99
  free association as fundamental rule in, 8, 99–100
  of group, 120–121, 122
  and healing mechanisms, 106–107
  and hypnosis, 116–117

initial interview for, 96–98
plasticity vs. rigidity in, 108–109
as form of psychotherapy, 115–124
short, 117–120
and theatrotherapy, 121–123
therapeutic achievements of, 104–106
transference in, 101–104
variations in, 108–114

Ulcer, peptic, 91, 92
Unconscious, 12, 16, 35, 36, 96
  collective, 11, 40
  and consciousness, 48–49
  and reality principle, 21
  repression into, 47

Vegetative neuroses, 90–92

Watson, John B., 24
Weaning, 30, 32
Wish fulfillment, in dreams, 56, 60, 64
Wit and Its Relation to the Unconscious (Freud), 9